HIDDEN FIELDS
A Guide for Workplace
Christian Fellowship Groups

by Ron Larson

DORRANCE PUBLISHING CO., INC.
PITTSBURGH, PENNSYLVANIA 15222

ISBN: 978-0-8059-7454-6
Printed in the United States of America

First Printing

For more information or to order additional books, please contact:
Dorrance Publishing Co., Inc.
701 Smithfield Street
Third Floor
Pittsburgh, Pennsylvania 15222
U.S.A.
1-800-788-7654
www.dorrancebookstore.com

"The harvest is plentiful but the workers are few. Ask the Lord of the harvest, therefore, to send out workers into his harvest field."

—Matthew 9:37-38 NIV

Dedication
To God the Father Almighty—
A precious gift received.

"Therefore, since we have this ministry, as we have received mercy, we do not lose heart."
—2 Corinthians 4:1

Acknowledgements

—God, for His calling of me
—Family, for their continuing support
—Workplace family, for their encouragement
—Janice LoBianco, as my personal editor

PREFACE

As a true believer in Jesus Christ as my Lord and Savior, I am committed to fulfilling God's command to bring others to know Him by accepting Jesus as their Lord and Savior. Therefore, my primary purpose for writing this book is twofold: 1) to capture my own life experiences in ministry to those in the workplace world, and 2) to challenge and encourage other believers to join in this ministry. Furthermore, the Holy Spirit has led me to write this book with the focus on enabling true believers to reach out to others in their own immediate workplace.

Every follower of Christ is ordained to be a minister, whether or not he or she acknowledges this gracious gift from God. Thus, it is each Christian's duty to go beyond being right with God. Just as important is working to gather others to Him. When I use the term *hidden fields* in this book, I refer to those places in everyday life that are overlooked as places of ministry to spread God's Word and to bring others to know Christ.

For too long, people have been conditioned by worldly values and rules dictating that God cannot be in the same place with other "non-religious" activities. Keeping God out of the workplace is an outgrowth of what is misunderstood to be separation of Church and State. It is time to break down these barriers. The fields are fertile. God is calling us with a sense of urgency to plant the seeds of salvation.

1

A CALLING

Having a job and working for a living is a necessary part of life for most of us. The example set by my parents and others around me demonstrated this reality. It doesn't matter today, however, if a man or woman is the breadwinner, since the old idea of male-only breadwinners has long passed away with our materialistic world. The general expectation of our culture and society is for people to go to school, get a good education, and enter the real world with a job for monetary support. Along with a job, an idealistic dream crops up as workers start to make more money than ever before—to gain the ability to posses anything and everything we desire. Then we may begin to think seriously of finding the right mate, leading us to be constantly reminded that if we want to have a family, we need a good job to support that family in a comfortable lifestyle.

All of these ideas and dreams came true for me. I felt satisfied that I met all expectations to take my rightful place in the world. I was independent and self-sufficient. I was a husband, a daddy, a respected worker, and my family lived a comfortable lifestyle. Thinking about going through this routine, working day after day for decades until I reach retirement (if I live that long), made me wonder: Is this picture of life in the workplace complete? Something still seemed hollow to me, but I really couldn't put my finger on what was missing.

The workplace, often referred to as the *marketplace*, is the environment where we spend much of our lives. Beginning a typical workday takes us more time than we would like in traveling to our work location. When we arrive, we prepare for the day's activities, either quietly by ourselves or by updating our lives with other co-workers. Then we dig into our work activities, sometimes with a renewed energy, and other times drudgingly. In the middle of the day, we try to grab something to eat and take a breather from the hectic pace. The remainder of the day goes quickly in a frantic rush to meet deadlines or daily goals, as our mental and physical energy continues to drain. We finally drag ourselves out the door to travel home or go to other committed activities. For *workaholics*, this may mean doing even more work at home. And during this daily routine, have we ever taken a moment to consider our spiritual health? What part does God have in all of this?

Consider for a moment how much time we spend in the workplace. It is probably much more than we would like to admit. Probably more time than our waking hours at home and much more than Church (unless this is your vocation) or any other activities we pursue. During all this time in the workplace, why do we seem to put our faith in the closet, keeping it out of view from others and away from our own consciousness? Maybe we are concerned about what others may think. Are we afraid to cross the line of acceptable business conduct? Or are we just lazy about making our faith a full-time endeavor, considering the workplace as an accepted place to have *time out* from all religious activities, commitments, and expectations? Entering the doors of our workplace for some of us is like leaving Jesus waiting outside while we are inside at work.

Since I came to Christ in the mid-1990's, I have personally struggled with these questions. I have, however, come to believe that it doesn't have to be this way. This really struck me during a leadership conference in 1998 at the Willow Creek Community Church in Barrington, Illinois, just west of Chicago. As chairperson of the board of trustees of our Church, I had been invited to attend this conference with several other key leaders from the Church. The mid-week New Community service that we attended, as in many Bible-based Churches, was not only a time for worship, but also a time for teaching and fellowship. In his message, the speaker related how he had previously worked in the urban Chicago metropolitan area. As a regular attendee of Willow Creek, he would rush home on the public transit system, just in time to make it to the mid-week service. Suddenly my attention to what he was saying came to a screeching halt. The immediate question that came to mind (or rather that God laid on my heart) was why does he, or the rest of us for that matter, have to go to a Church to find Christian fellowship and teaching? Why can't we do the same things in the workplace, not intending to replace Church but to extend our Christian lives from *part-time* to *full- time*?

For the remainder of the service, I didn't remember hearing any more of his message. I found myself looking upward at the ceiling and around the large auditorium, which seats over 5,000 people. I was tuned out to everything that was happening around me. I began to sense that something special was happening, something I had never been conscious of experiencing before. Through the power of the Holy Spirit, God had my attention. When the message for the evening ended and the praise team closed the service, I just sat there in my seat. I remember that some of those with our Church group looked at me with an uncertain look. As I got up and left the auditorium, it was almost like I was floating across the floor, and all I could do was smile.

This was the most powerful moment of the conference, and possibly my entire Christian life. Call it a revelation, an epiphany, or something else; I have never been so touched by something in my life. I felt a sense of awe, excitement, wonder, anxiety, obedience, and doubt, all at the same time. I think the sensation of doubt stemmed from second-guessing what I had heard and what it meant. The doubt was not eased by sharing this experience with others in our group. I had difficulty putting my feelings into words, and as a result, none of them seemed too interested in listening to what I had to say. Nonetheless, I knew God was working in my life in some special way.

After returning home to Clearwater, Florida, from the conference, I realized the longer I reflected on this message about a spiritual calling, the more it made perfect sense. The workplace, where we spend so much of our time, would be a great place for ministry and for continuing to nourish one's spirit in fellowship with co-workers—a captive audience that is spiritually equal resides there without denominational barriers. In a Church, all who come to worship and serve make that conscious decision to walk through the front doors. But in the workplace, people are present every day of the week as a matter of necessity. The workplace is an untapped source of people who need the love of Christ, regardless of where they are in their spiritual walk. These are the hidden fields, fertile for nurturing and growth.

Most of us are familiar with the phrase "What Would Jesus Do?" or WWJD? It is a good question to ask, as we look to God's Word for direction. As recorded in the gospels, when Jesus gathered His disciples, where did he find them? As best we know, Jesus did not go looking for them at the temple or synagogue. Instead, Jesus found His disciples in the common man's workplace. Four of them were fisherman: Andrew, Simon Peter, James, and John. Matthew was a tax collector. Even Judas Iscariot was thought to be a bookkeeper. These were men of various backgrounds and possibly of different beliefs. The one element they had in common were jobs in which they worked for a living. So why have we now become ignorant of the fact that we can live our faith in the workplace? Does scripture tell us that we have to quit our jobs to follow Christ? Unfortunately, the spiritually sterile workplace has become a cultural norm where any mention of faith or religion is not politically or morally correct. What a way to distance ourselves from God!

In my response to this calling from God, I began a search for what others have written that would offer me some guidance and insight. There are many Christian books and publications available today which focus on our relationship with God in the workplace or *marketplace*. Most of these books deal with Christians living out their lives in the *marketplace* in the way God commands them to be as followers of Christ. These authors address key traits such as serving, integrity, trust, character, and skill as workers fulfill the expectations of their job and deal with others in the corporate scheme. All of these resources provide a great guide to our own relationship with and within the *corporate structure*.

Few authors, however, have dealt significantly with day-to-day direct relationships with co-workers, in the same way they interact with others at home and with their Christian walk. I think the key word here is *marketplace*, which can be misconstrued in the classic sense as meaning a buyer-seller connection. Even in our own immediate workplace, we are either receiving service from another to meet our expectations (buyer) or we are serving to satisfy the expectations of someone else (selling). This could be a supervisor/subordinate relationship in the business world or a teacher/student relationship in a school setting. Whatever the situation, these relationships are not one-on-one on a peer or equal basis. As Christians, we are not buyers or sellers in the relationships we have with co-workers—we are directly connected in the common bonds of Christ.

So what *is* available for Christians to use as a guide for encouragement to strengthen relationships and faith in the workplace? I believe that this Christian workplace ministry is what God has laid on my heart to share in this book. Even though I am not a formally educated theologian, and have little experience in ministry, God is equipping me for this endeavor. I am only an instrument in God's hands. These are not my words, but words God speaks through me to touch the hearts and minds of others.

2
PREPARATION

Not long after I accepted Jesus Christ into my life, during a rush of insatiable hunger for God's Word, I participated in a fellowship study called *Experiencing God¹*. This was not so much a Bible study of God's Word, but a guide to understanding what a one-on-one relationship with God really means. This study, which I highly recommend to others, opened my eyes to what God wants for me—to listen to His calling and direction and to join Him in His work. As with many circumstances in life, we only realize God's works after they happen by looking back to see what He has done. Looking back at my past, I know this was, and is, His plan for me.

I suppose that if I had known Christ when I began working over twenty-five years ago, I might not have really recognized or fully appreciated the need for ministry in the workplace. It's like the "forest for the trees" perspective, where I may have been too close and involved in the workplace world to see all the lost people. But this was not God's plan for me. God wanted me to experience the workplace first, for twenty-five years, to know the true condition of the human spirit in the workplace. It is place where time, money, and organization rules, a place where the expectations and stress can literally break a person's will and spirit, not to mention their physical well-being, and a place where any mention or reference to one's own spiritual faith is either considered unacceptable (crossing the line) or as a sign of weakness. My twenty-five years of experience was a part of God's plan for me. In hindsight, I know I am stronger now and more prepared to continue in His work.

My first twenty-five years in the workplace began with my graduation from college with an electrical engineering degree. Although not prompted by my father, who was also an electrical engineer, I chose this field of study because I always wondered what my father did at work. My interest in those objective subjects such as math and science, which revolve around a problem and solution mentality, nicely supported the engineering curriculum. This mentality, however, was also a curse for my spiritual life. Everything had to have a logical explanation. I was a problem solver. I was in control, or so I thought. There was no room in my life for faith or trust in something unseen.

Throughout my working career, much of my time was spent designing and managing projects. There were, however, instances when I was required to spend time in the field at project sites to monitor construction progress, review operating and maintenance programs, and witness testing of systems and equipment. One lengthy full-time assignment was held at a project site for two and one half years. In another position as a manager for several years in a large manufacturing facility, I was constantly interfacing with production workers from the beginning to the end of the production process. All of these opportunities were part of God's preparatory plan for me. By direct immersion into the heart of the workplace, I gained an acute awareness of many different workplace environments and the human condition of each.

From a spiritual perspective, I am a person with little religious background. I went to Church as a kid because it was the expected practice and made my mother satisfied and happy. In my high school and college years, Church or any form of a religious life became foreign to me. I *did* believe that there was a God, but that belief pretty much ended there. At one time, I even referred to myself as an *agnostic*, out of laziness to explore what God is all about, and as a defense to any questions others may have directed at me about my faith. After marrying and having children, I reluctantly returned to the Church scene with the attitude that as a responsible parent, it was the right thing to do. My rationale was that Church would expose my kids to religion so they could make up their own minds about their faith as they became older (my engineer's decision-making persona being imposed on my kids). This lasted about as long as my youngest child, Abby, was in grade school, when we gradually backslid to be free again of the religious obligation for the balance of those first twenty-five years in the workplace. I think many people can truthfully relate a similar background of their walk (or lack thereof) in faith.

In 1995, God's plan for my life entered its next phase. Through a series of events and circumstances, I accepted Jesus Christ as my Lord and Savior. This relationship was something I had never known before. For me, acceptance of Christ was not a specific timed or dated event but it evolved over several months as Christ drew me closer and closer to Him. Then at one point in time, I really knew I was His when I found myself professing Jesus to others. I had surrendered all that I am to Him. The close one-on-one relationship I developed with God through knowing Jesus gave me comfort and a sense of peace I had never known before. This peace led me to a level of self-confidence and excitement that literally propelled me to tell others of God's grace and love. Beyond my home, Church, and community, I considered nothing off limits, not even my workplace. But little did I know what a challenge it would be to witness and find Christian fellowship in the workplace. I soon understood that God had prepared me for this ministry, armed with a new self-confidence and boldness to meet this challenge. This was all in

6

God's timing and plan, as best captured by the Apostle Paul when he wrote to the Church at Corinth about his calling "as one born out of due time" (1 Corinthians 15:8)

Promise Keepers[2] provided another major spiritual influence in my life. The ministry provided by this organization was one of the key elements contributing to my coming to Christ. In addition, the fellowship opportunities provided at large conferences and small group gatherings opened my eyes to the real human and sensitive side of other men. Below that rough exterior of all men there exists a heart that can be opened to the love of other men through Christ. Even though there are both men and women in the workplace, as a man I know that the hearts of other men are the toughest to open up to receive God's message. This preparation was just another element in God's plan for me.

One Step at a Time

Another example of God's preparation of my life is really remarkable and blatantly obvious. I related in the last chapter how my attendance at the leadership conference occurred because of my position as chairperson of the board of trustees. Three years earlier, when I had only been attending that Church for about one year and had only recently realized that I had accepted Christ into my life, a member of the Church approached me. He asked if I would be willing to have my name included as a nominee for the board of trustees. I was surprised since I had only been with the Church, one of 2000+ members, for only a short time. Nevertheless, I accepted this invitation since I expected to be one of several names, one most people would not be familiar with, and one that would fill out a list with no real expectation of being called to serve. Little did I know at the time that the leadership only acquires enough committed nominees to fill out the available positions. Needless to say, when I attended the Church's annual business meeting, I was surprised to find myself automatically swept up in role of service. This was God's first step for me.

Two years later, I was beginning my third of a three-year position on the board of trustees. We were having our first meeting for the new year one evening and I was running a little late. As I walked in the door, I apologized for being late. As I settled in my seat, I noticed most of the members staring at me with sheepish grins on their faces. When I asked what was going on, one of them said, "We've been waiting for you." In response to my question "why" they indicated that they had agreed before I arrived that they wanted me to the chairperson of the board for the next year; to be honest I had never even entertained the idea. Without much hesitation, but a little humorous banter about this decision process, I graciously accepted the position. In hindsight, I know now that God had provided this second step in His plan for me. His third step provided the opportunity several months later to attend a leadership conference as the leader representing the board of trustees. Step by step, He has created a plan for me, just as He does for all of us.

Since coming to Christ and recognizing God's calling, I have wondered how essential it is to have a formal theological training. I have felt at times that to be part of any ministry, some formal training is a prerequisite to be accepted as credible. When I discussed my ministry with other pastoral and ministry staff at Churches I have attended, I always walked away with a feeling of inadequacy. My only real training has been life experience and my own constant study of God's Word through other fellowship Bible studies. As I read God's word, I am frequently reminded of others God used as his earthly instruments, who considered themselves unprepared or equipped for God's plan. Moses is one commonly recognized example from the Old Testament, as he pleaded his own case before God with a feeling of inadequacy and a sense of being unprepared. In the New Testament, I am reminded of the original twelve disciples. Did Jesus choose them because they had any significant religious training? From scripture we don't really know if they did. If they had, and it was an important factor in their ministry, wouldn't God have revealed this to us in His Word? These disciples did have the greatest teacher we know on this earth in Jesus, but they were essentially common people who were destined in God's plan to minister to others. In a similar way, these examples provide me, a common man, the courage and validation to pursue this ministry that God has prepared for me to share.

3
PRAYER

I am not an expert on prayer, but God has gifted others to communicate His Word to us about the reasons why we should pray, when we should pray, where we should pray, and what expectations we should have from prayer. If nothing else, we should truly understand and accept that He wants us to pray. My only expertise about prayer stems from my own personal experience as I have responded to Him. Definitely, prayer has changed my life and solidified my personal one-on-one relationship with God. I am a true believer that prayer should precede any endeavor I undertake in life. With His calling of me to this workplace ministry, prayer has become an essential first step.

Two-Way

Throughout the recorded ages, much has been written and spoken about prayer. The Gospels of Matthew 6 and Luke 11 relate how Jesus taught the disciples, and all of us for that matter, how we should pray. By the example and words of Jesus, we know we need to make prayer a priority in our lives. Regardless of one's religion or faith, prayer is an essential element in one's relationship with God. There may be a misconception by some; that prayer is only a one-way dialog *from* us *to* God. Prayer is in fact a two-way communication, or communion, with God. As we open ourselves in prayer to our Heavenly Father, we must be ever conscious of the times that God wants to speak to us. At these times, we must quietly listen to what He will lay on our hearts. Although prayer has been a significant part of my life ever since I accepted Christ, it took me a while before I really learned to be still and listen to Him. Even now, I continue to struggle with myself to allow for those quiet times and places so God may enter my heart. When James writes for us to be "quick to listen, slow to speak" (James 1:19), his instruction applies to more than our earthly communication with others. It should also remind us of spirit-filled moments in which we commune with or listen to God through prayer.

Although I know that God directs my involvement in this workplace ministry, He has not given me a written invitation or game plan to follow. There are times, however, that I know God has provided me direction through His Word and my life circumstances. The most significant proof of God's faithfulness is the direction He has given me through prayer, especially as I become obediently still and listen to Him. A true example of this occurs when I am focused on lifting up my daily prayers to God, when all of a sudden I am abruptly interrupted. It's like when you are watching television and without warning you hear, *"We interrupt the regular scheduled programming for this important message...."* I know that it's God telling me to quit talking and give Him some time to speak to me. As I've learned to recognize these moments, I'm in awe of His power and plan for me. His direction for me, when I am obedient to follow Him, has impacted my life and this ministry in ways that I could have never imagined.

Never underestimate the power of prayer. Jim Cymbala, the pastor of Brooklyn Tabernacle in New York, has expressed this idea in a sincerely heartfelt way in his book *Fresh Wind, Fresh Fire*[3]. After responding to a calling of the spirit to become pastor at Brooklyn Tabernacle, Jim was losing ground in an attempt to revive the Church. None of his efforts seemed to produce results. Then, during a much-needed time of vacation in St. Petersburg, Florida, Jim felt God speaking to his heart. By turning things over to God through persistent prayer, wondrous things happened. Today his Church is one of the largest in the New York area, and prayer continues to be the first priority of this Church, especially at the mid-week prayer meetings. God *does* want to have a close personal relationship with each of us; prayer is the essential key to being part of His plan. For me, nothing is more fulfilling than seeing answered prayers. We may not see everything happen that we pray for, but His plan will be clearly revealed to us in His own time.

Where/When

Jesus told his disciples, "When you pray, go into your room, close the door and pray to your Father, who is unseen" (Matthew 6:6). Finding a quiet place to pray, away from the hectic pace and distractions of daily life, can be difficult. But the hardest part of the struggle is to intentionally devote time for prayer. I have actually discovered, however, that the daily routine at my workplace, which is fairly disciplined in contrast to the other aspects of my life, offers more time and places to pray than I would have imagined. When I drive to work in the mornings, I make a point of keeping the radio and my cell phone off. Except for the drone of the traffic outside, I find the quiet interior of my car to be a sanctuary to speak with God and to listen to Him. Although my prayers may be occasionally interrupted by my needed attention to driving,

God doesn't care if we talk to Him in parts, as long as we just talk to Him. Whether we drive ourselves to work or use public transportation, each of us will surprisingly find a good amount of time to commune with God.

I have made it a point in the past few years to finish my morning prayers and communion with God at the office. To avoid the heavy rush hour traffic, I usually leave for work earlier than necessary. This affords me the extra time when I reach my workplace before the daily demands begin. With the luxury of having an office with a door that can be closed, I spend time praying; and usually finish with God speaking to me through scriptures. Although I have not said anything to anyone concerning this time, many co-workers have come to know that this is my quiet time and respect it by not interrupting me. If someone does knock or just walks in, however, I assure him that he has not interrupted me, for I know it is God's intention for me to redirect my focus to the one who has entered. In fact, prayer is one of the greatest witnessing tools available to us. Also, I know that anyone seeking to find a secluded place and time for devotion can succeed since anything is possible with God.

The more times we turn ourselves to the Lord in prayer each day, the more constant our focus is on God. Someone once told me about what he referred to as "popcorn prayers." These are short, maybe one-sentence prayers that we lift up to God during our daily situations. Examples are, "Lord, I'm going to be traveling to work in this rush hour traffic, please give me a safe journey," or "Father, I'm starting to do a large, two-sided copying job, so please make it go smoothly and give me the patience to deal with any problems I may have with the copy machine," or "God, I just finished digging this trench with my backhoe, thank you for not hitting the water and gas lines that I knew were buried somewhere below." With the picture of popcorn, I have visualized these prayers in another way. Consider for a moment how a bag of uncooked microwave popcorn looks—flat, in a plain wrapper, kernels in a mixture of the artificial butter—overall it looks disgusting, as our lives may be sometimes. Then consider how each one of the raw corn kernels represents a situation in our daily lives and how the bag reflects our own spirit. As we lift up prayers to God for each daily situation, it's almost as if each raw kernel being popped represents the fulfilling power of the Holy Spirit, invisible to us, but ever present. The more prayers we lift up, the fuller the bag gets, until it is bursting with fullness and a pleasing aroma. How filled our own spirits become during each day reflects how diligently we speak with God.

Being Bold

Ever since I have given my life to Christ to become bold and confident in my walk of faith, I have not been hesitant to turn to the Lord in prayer. For example, I pray before all meals; I don't mean just at home, but also in public places. Whether eating with others or by myself, I am not ashamed to bow my head and give thanks to the Lord for providing everything with which He has blessed me. In fact, my family knows my ways and expects me to pray with them whenever and wherever we share a meal together. At one time in my life, I even tested this expectation when some of our family was having dinner at a restaurant with some of their friends for a birthday celebration. Not knowing the wishes of their friends to join in prayer together, I chose to bow my head and pray silently. In a moment, I heard a cry from one of the friends who wanted to be included in the prayer. I looked up and everyone was staring at me in amazement. Then and there, I learned more fully of the power of prayer and the effect it has on people's lives.

During an extended work assignment out of town, one of my business associates, Dave, noticed that I silently prayed before eating when we were dining with a group of other associates. He approached me one-on-one after the meal and said how awesome it was to see me be bold enough to pray in public. Although my motive was only to give thanks to God, this outward display of my faith had touched him, and it led to further discussions of our own walks of faith. With continued encouragement and support, Dave is now guiding Christian fellowship in another one of our corporate offices.

Being bold enough to pray openly in the presence of others is one of the greatest ways of witnessing our faith. In doing so, our prayers should be heartfelt and not for the purpose of saying what we think others want to hear. Many of us have been in gatherings, with one or more persons, where we have all prayed together. As we listen to others praying out loud, they may seem to be struggling with what to say or to express. We almost feel sympathetically critical of how they are speaking and we want to help them. At these times, we must be sure to remember that their prayer ability is not for us to judge. Some people are eloquent in speaking, others are not. How are we to know what is on the hearts of other people? As Paul writes in Romans 8:26, "When you pray, it is better to have a heart without words, than words without a heart." Worse than struggling with prayer, however, is not to pray at all. Sometimes at the beginning or end of a business meeting in the workplace, I feel emptiness because prayer is not part of the agenda. For me, a brief silent prayer to our Father in Heaven fills that void.

A Common Need

Seeing such power in prayer, our workplace fellowship group has made prayer the one true foundation in this ministry. Those in our workplace have come to know that our fellowship group will pray for any situation. If we hear of some condition, we will ask the individual if it is okay to include it in our prayers. Almost every day, one of our group members is approached by a co-worker or will receive a written message (e.g. e-mail) to add someone or some situation to our prayer list. We have made it a point to pray for individuals who may be leaving us to undergo surgery, coming together for a brief moment to pray for that individual while their surgery is being performed. In fact, one of the most awesome things to happen in our workplace was the willingness of our company management to allow for a time of prayer several days after the September 11, 2001 tragedy. As a result, new faces joined our group, enlarging the number of workers to gather the harvest in the field.

I can't ever remember a time when someone said they did not want or need our prayers. Even a proclaimed atheist in our workplace, who is outwardly vocal of his non-belief and displeasure of our workplace fellowship, openly accepted our offers of prayer for his wife as she was to undergo serious cancer surgery. Maybe he was "hedging his bets." Regardless of one's walk in faith or chosen religious denomination, I believe that deep inside everyone, the mystery and power of prayer resides. Prayer is indeed one primary foundation of our faith, so keep on praying.

4

A GATHERING

In late 1997, I found myself making a conscious effort to seek other Christians in my workplace to joyfully share my newfound faith, and to find the comfort that I knew true Christian fellowship could offer. Through my casual conversations during the course of the workday, I would "throw out the bait" to see if I got any bites. Jesus commanded His disciples to "come follow me, and I will make you fishers of men" (Matthew 4:19). So, too, I was fishing to identify those around me who, by their words and/or actions, showed me that their faith was an important life factor. Small things I said, such as inquiring about what Church someone went to, or making comments about my Church activities, usually provided a flag of *go* or *no go* in pursuing the matter any further. Expressing a sincere interest in the situations of others and asking if I could pray for them also revealed levels of faith and desires for further dialog. It was amazing how well these interactions worked with a sensitive approach and very few confrontations with non-believers.

This dialog was great as a first step, but the small tidbits of time we could find to converse and share with one another, while honoring the job demands, left me with an unsatisfied feeling. It felt similar to having the opportunity to interview someone I really admired, but only being able to ask that person one question. I felt frustrated. How we could spend more time together became a real dilemma. As I struggled with this issue, I began to ask others about their thoughts and interest in setting aside a special time for gathering together as a group. Although I was initiating this dialog, I was not one to normally step forward to lead a group, especially since I was still an infant in my faith walk. In biblical literacy, I was just a beginner. Yet, as others expressed what appeared to be a genuine interest in the idea, I felt God telling me that since no one else has stepped forward, I should take the bold step to do it myself. I can honestly say that this time I really followed divine guidance. So in February of 1998, I arranged for our first meeting in the early morning, an hour before our official starting time of work. With expectancy I wondered if anyone would really come.

Now that we had set a time and place, the idea of what we were going to do during our time together dawned on me. Each of us could spend some time sharing about our families, faith backgrounds, and any needs that could be lifted up in prayer, but would this fill up an hour of our time together? Should we do some type of Bible study? What about the next meeting, and then the next? Through this entire mental struggle, I forgot one important thing: to put my trust in God. Isn't He the one who brought this opportunity about in the first place? Isn't He the one who was prompting and guiding me by His direction? I had to remind myself that this was His plan and His timing. Immediately, I put those words on my computer as a screen saver, and to this day I still have them as a constant reminder.

A Beginning

We first began to meet early in the morning one day a week in one of our workplace conference rooms, an hour before the start of the workday. With four or five of us together, I think I wasn't the only one who was wondering how we would spend our time together. I brought in some reference material by Christian authors, with the primary direction towards how we should model ourselves as Christians in the workplace. We briefly reviewed this material, but quickly turned away from focusing on any structured study and found ourselves discussing our own life circumstances and feelings. Some shared personal trials with which they were struggling, both in and outside of the workplace. Others related concerns that needed to be lifted up in prayer. Even current events happening in our local and global world and how we should relate to these events as Christians became food for discussion. Regardless of each of our own levels of faith, a genuine heartfelt sense of fellowship and trust began to develop within our group. I thought to myself, *This is what it is all about; caring for others.* What a great commandment Jesus gave us with "Love each other as I have loved you" (John 15:12).

As time went on, over weeks and months of meeting together, we rarely had a structured plan to our meetings. Most meetings would take on a different form. Another person would bring up a topic or share an article from some publication that we would discuss as it related to our Christian walk. Someone had a question about life circumstances that prompted us to dig into the Bible for scriptural references and direction from God's Word. For a period of time, one person brought in a series of videos that we watched, walking us through the Bible and referencing the setting of the biblical events as they related to Israel in the current times. In every meeting, we also devoted an open time for sharing and prayer. Many times we were astonished at how quickly our time together passed, leaving us with a longing to continue. This, in itself, helped us all to learn the meaning of *honor*, that of respecting our workplace commitments by returning to our work activities in the prescribed time.

Over the course of our first six months of meeting together, it became a struggle for some of our group members to get to work an extra hour early, even for only one day a week. The human will is very powerful, especially when one can get an extra hour of sleep. There were others who would have come to our meetings, but family scheduling circumstances, such at transporting their kids to school, made them unable to do so. Thus, it became apparent that we needed a time change. Meeting after work, however, would present similar obstacles. The only other real choice was to meet during the lunch hour. What a revelation! It was so obvious that I almost felt shamefully stupid. Why does scripture so frequently relate times of fellowship over meals, such as when Jesus eats with tax collectors and others (Acts 2:46), and when the jailer in Philippi invited Paul and Silas to his house to share a meal after the jailer received Christ into his life (Acts 16:34)? The lunch hour is a time when everyone needs to take a break, to rest and physically replenish his or her body. It is also a time to replenish one's mind and heart in the spirit. To this day, we continue to meet during the lunch hour. We even refer to our gathering as "The Lunch Group" (with more on the background of this label to be addressed in Chapter 7, *A Fine Line*).

In retrospect, we discovered that trying to set one meeting time and place cannot satisfy everyone. Each individual has his or her own scheduling priorities, as well as commitments set by others, which are beyond their control. I do continue to include in my prayers those who do have a choice in adjusting their own schedules: may they make God a priority in their lives and make this lunchtime opportunity available for them to join our group.

Another Step

With a meeting time and place set, the other major hurdle encompassed the encouragement of people to come and then to provide them a reminder so they wouldn't forget. When we first started meeting as a group of six or eight, it was relatively easy to give a personal face-to-face invitation and reminder to each person. As more and more people expressed an interest in our group, however, this personal touch became unwieldy and time consuming. So we began to prepare and distribute written reminders. This offered an added benefit of sharing an inspirational thought, referencing a timely scripture, and providing an active prayer list. We were even graced with requests by persons who, although not interested in being part of our group, wanted us to add someone or some situation to our prayer list.

God does work in awesome ways: something in my Church's reminders caught my attention, having a powerful impact on the distribution of our meeting reminders. Dennis and Barbara Rainey have co-authored a book called *Moments Together for Couples*.[4] In their book, they present a set of sixty weekly handouts of devotionals by the same title, which can be purchased at most Christian bookstores and are intended by copyright for limited reproduction/distribution. Although generally focused on the relationships of couples, these devotionals apply as well to family and relationships. Even though the majority of those who receive our weekly reminders do not choose to attend our group, the inclusion of these devotionals with our reminders has been a wonderful ministry tool. People look forward to receiving them and comment on how they have been *right on* for situations they may be facing in life. In fact, the first time we reached the end of distributing all sixty weeks of these devotionals, the general consensus was to begin again, which we have done several times. I would like to take this opportunity to offer thanks and a prayer of gratitude to the Raineys for the powerful message they are sharing with others. It has truly been a blessing to this ministry.

In mid-2003, after we had recycled the *Moments Together for Couples* devotional two additional times, it was time to move on with our own weekly messages. From a habit of writing a brief (e.g. one paragraph) inspirational message in each of our weekly reminder handouts, I felt that God was touching my heart to do more. One Sunday afternoon after Church, I wrote the first full column message (intended to be three duplicate copies to a page). I knew then, as I know now, that it wasn't me writing this message; it was the Holy Spirit working through me to physically put the words into print. Ever since the beginning of these writings, I look forward to what the Holy Spirit will place on my heart each week, and I am eager to acknowledge the authorship of the spirit to others, as they inquire about or commend these messages. In early 2004, I began to share these same messages to others outside of my workplace via e-mail distribution, under the title *The Fine Line*. Then, in late 2004, with a full year (e.g. fifty-two, one for each week) of these messages completed, I began to consider them published in a similar intended reproduction/distribution fashion as *Moments Together for Couples*, under the same title of *The Fine Line*. And this was not the end: more messages were to come.

Keeping Things Fresh

As the old saying goes, "You can't please all of the people all of the time." That is so true when it comes to meeting together in fellowship. There have been times when the interests of those attending our group have waned. Each person is unique, with different interests and on different levels of growth in his or her faith. Some like structured biblical teaching; some are more driven by the objective facts about history, archeology, science, and world events, while others just prefer a more *touchy-feely* time of sharing and prayer. How did we satisfy everyone without just giving up? As God's Word tells us, "Let us not give up meeting together, as some are in the habit of doing, but let us encourage one another—and all the more as you see the Day approaching" (Hebrews 10:25). If all things are placed in God's hands through prayer, He will show the way. First of all, we had to make sure we continued coming together in fellowship on a regular basis. Then, with an attitude and discipline for listening (James 1:19) to our group, our heartfelt needs became clearly evident. We set up a calendar of discussion times and topics, mixing types of interests throughout our meeting times, and shared this with everyone so they would know what to expect. We had to be creative, accommodating, and think outside the box. We used study resources that many of us had explored in our own Churches, and we made use of the talents of others in our group to lead topical discussions. Not everyone wanted to be involved in everything, but we guarded ourselves from becoming discouraged. The worst thing we could do was nothing! And in the end, our efforts, guided by God, generated a renewed energy to our group for attending and being involved.

As God is our rock and foundation, we can trust in Him to always be there; *never* changing. He is the constant measure on which we can rely in a world that is *ever* changing. Accordingly, the structure and form of fellowship gatherings needs to be flexible, to bend with life's circumstances, and yet it always needs to be focused on God. We can study the Bible, watch videos, discuss current events, and share personal situations and concerns, but if we are not careful, we achieve that *feel good* feeling without offering any substance. Personally, I have been critical of the approaches many Churches take today trying to deliver God's message in a user-friendly fashion that doesn't offend; otherwise, those receiving the message might not return. In the same way, I have caught myself doing the same thing in our workplace gatherings, being so anxious and determined to gather people together that I felt a need to please everyone all the time. We must remember that the message is not about what people *want* to hear, but what they *need to* hear. I thank God that He has put individuals in my path who have pulled me back in the right direction. One of them was bold enough to repeat to me a statement I had heard many times before, *The main thing is to keep the main thing the main thing*. All I can say to that is. *Amen.*

5
FAMILY

Since I am not formally educated or trained in many of the family issues that I will discuss here, especially *the family unit*, I would refer you to experts such as Dr. James Dobson, a person whom I highly admire and respect. The founder of the Christian based Focus on the Family Ministry, Dr. Dobson is highly qualified on many matters related to the family. Neither Dr. Dobson nor I have any formal theological training; but we do share God's calling and direction in doing His work. My only expertise in family issues is through trial by fire: being married for thirty-four years, raising three beautiful children, and being part of the workplace for over thirty-two years. From this experience I see a valid comparison of the similarities between values of the family in the common household and those of the family in the workplace.

What does the term *family* mean? Each one of us became a family member the day of our birth. The woman who bore us required the partnership of a man, thus giving us a mother and a father. If our mother and father have other children, they are our brothers and/or sisters. Each of us, if it be God's will, may have our own children to form another family unit. This life cycle can go on indefinitely, until no further offspring are produced and all of the remaining family members are no longer alive. This is how many people think of families. There is much more to being a family, however, than in this biological or genealogical sense.

Family is in itself a communion of two or more people, living and sharing their lives together. Webster's dictionary defines the word *family* as "a group of individuals living under one roof and usually one head of household."[5] Notice that this definition makes no reference to any biological connection of those living in the same household. For example, an adopted person is considered part of that family even though he or she is not of that family's direct biological lineage. Except for Christ, who is the only direct lineage to God as His son, God "predestined us to be adopted as his sons [and daughters] through Jesus Christ" (Ephesians 1:5). Thus, we are all part of God's family, being His adopted children. Even the criminal world offers another example of family. Many of the accepted members of a criminal organization consider themselves to be part of the family, caring for one another, although possibly in the pursuit of evil. As a contrary example, a person of direct biological lineage who leaves a household, such as in the extreme case of being rejected and ostracized, may not be considered as part of the family. In any case, the primary focus of the family is for the common good of all in the group.

A Family that Works Together

With an understanding of what a family really is, most of us would agree that a family is what normally dwells within most homes. Looking beyond the walls of our homes, a true sense of family can also be seen in many Church communities, where members exemplify sincere commitment to sharing and caring for others. Being "part of the family" may also be the reference in social clubs, etc. But how often do we ever refer to being part of the family in our workplace? The rigid structure of the corporate world often tends to stifle any fostering of the closeness that a family unit can provide. Especially where clients and customers are concerned, getting too close can be seen as unprofessional, or as not being a good business practice. Maybe this is why the classic stance in the medical profession is for doctors not to get too close to their patients. Personally, I have been confronted by my own management about getting too close to clients, when my manager perceived that I was attempting to be accepted as "part of a client's family." Ironically, a short time later, the same manager referred to one of his long time clients as "family." When I reminded him of my situation, all he could say was "touché."

In most workplaces, the business enterprise consists of more than one person. As such, personal relationships must exist for the business to function. These relationships serve as the core of the workplace group, just as they do in a household family. We live together for much of our time on this earth, we experience trials and pain together, and we celebrate in the joy of good times together. Regardless of the type or form of our workplace environment and regardless of how many different jobs we may have over a lifetime, each workplace is still like a family unit through our common business relationship. Therefore, denying that family community bonds exist in the workplace is a fallacy.

For each one of us who have ever worked as part of a group, whether as a paid employee or as a volunteer, we have probably experienced many human emotions, not only with ourselves, but also with others in the group. In our own experiences, we have probably seen the physical pain of others stemming from health problems. We have also shared the emotional pains of others, such as going through a divorce, or losing a close relative or friend through illness. We might have comforted another person who has been given notice that they will no longer be working for the company and may be in a state of shock and disbelief. On the other hand, we probably have also shared with others the joy of celebrating birthdays, getting married, having a new baby, getting a promotion and being part of company gatherings, such as picnics and Christmas parties. With all these commonly shared life circumstances and relationships, it is hard to believe that the workplace is not synonymous with a family structure.

Some of the special memories I recall of these family relationships in my workplace include:

- Visiting a co-worker and his wife in the hospital a day after the birth of their first child, and being asked to pray with them to praise God and give thanks for her birth.
- The "laying on of hands" to pray with other coworkers for one of our own who was about to undergo surgery and a lengthy recovery process.
- Being with a co-worker to witness his baptism after he accepted Christ.
- Comforting a co-worker when he was released from the company and staying in close contact with him to give him encouragement and moral support during the time it took for him to find new employment.
- Saying goodbye to a co-worker at his retirement, knowing that at the time he had not accepted Christ, but had faithfully been part of our workplace fellowship group for several years.
- Attending the funeral of a co-worker, who at the young age of thirty-five years, died from a heart attack, leaving a wife and four sons under the age of ten.

As I was recalling and listing these situations, it became apparent to me that they encompassed the complete cycle of life, from birth to death, and all that is in between. Life in the workplace is not a sterile, emotionless place, but a part of the dynamic fiber of life, ever alive and thriving throughout the busy workday routine.

Another example of the workplace family stems from my wife Marilou, who manages a local office of a national corporation, overseeing a staff of approximately fifteen to twenty men and women of diverse ages and backgrounds. She usually shares with me the daily circumstances she faces, not only about work production and corporate issues, but also about the human side of managing her staff. In doing so, she not only gets feedback from me to validate her actions, but also suggestions she might consider using in the future. I look forward to her sharing workplace experiences with me because it offers me another perspective on a second workplace environment. The one clear and common thread between our two workplaces is the obvious presence of the family unit. Her staff sees Marilou as a person who is in control as an effective manager in the pursuit of their business goals. She is perceived as being fair with her staff, but will rapidly act on any situation that is not in the best interests of the group. For example, she will not tolerate whining or confrontation of authority that would be classified as insubordination. In this way, she has been very successful in achieving a strong business ethic, while maintaining a close-knit personal staff that enjoys working for her and with her. Some of the younger staff even lovingly and respectfully refer to her as "Mom."

Who's in Charge?

Over the course of recent times, we have seen an increase in the level of independence being demonstrated by today's youth. This may be through the encouragement of their parents, or by necessity stemming from the lack of attention or guidance by their parents. In either case, this independence has led to feelings by youth of *being in control*, with some resulting lack of tolerance and respect for authority. In turn, this poses difficulty for parents in maintaining a close household family unit, where youth want to escape parental authority, causing the household family unit to struggle to survive. The workplace, on the other hand, has not and will not succumb to accepting workers *being in control* on their own accord, if it wants to survive.

As a family unit, the workplace *does* still maintain the respect and authority that the general model of a household family used to have. I have seen some of our youth enter the workplace in recent years, and it is discouraging that a significant percentage of them don't succeed as a result of their expectations of being in control and wanting to change the world. They have lost the true core values of accepting authority. Maybe this is one of the reasons why many high school and college graduates who enter the workplace try it for a while, and then return home to live with their parents for financial reasons, since they are having difficulty maintaining employment.

When a faith-based fellowship is available to the youth in the workplace, it can offer a reality check in a sincere and loving way. Before these youth, who have so much energy and potential "hit the wall" in frustration and failure, others may come along side to guide and mentor them. The workplace family is not meant to replace their own personal family connections. Fortunately, it is there to help reveal to them God's love and ultimate plan for their lives.

In summary, the workplace environment functions as a family unit. Therefore, as we all learn more about family values through God's Word, our own life experiences, and from trained experts on the subject, let us be reminded that these issues apply more than just to our family at home. We are one family of God's children: wherever we come together in communion with one another.

6

PLANTING

For any field to ever become fruitful, one must plant the seeds that only God can provide. And in order for those seeds to grow and flourish, they must be planted in fertile soil, watered, and receive the warmth and radiance of light. We have all seen the miracle of seedlings growing into flowers, grass, trees, and garden vegetables. When I was in early grade school, I can remember a teacher giving each of us a paper cup and several seeds that were supposed to grow into a plant that had pea pods. We filled the cup with potting soil, pushed our finger into the soil to make a hole for the seeds, dropped the seeds in, and covered them with dirt. Finally, we added the right amount of water and placed our cup on the sunny window ledge of the schoolroom, trusting that in time, a plant would grow.

When I think of planting seeds that lead to a life in Christ, I frequently recall the parable of the farmer planting seeds (God's Word) that Jesus relates to the people in Luke 8:5-8. We see the importance of this lesson because Jesus takes the time to explain the meaning of this parable to His Disciples for their clear understanding (Luke 8:11-15). God doesn't want us to waste our time by wildly planting seeds and then ignoring them, hoping that seedlings will sprout on their own. Our job mirrors that of the farmer, who must nurture and cultivate the seeds he plants, right up until the time the fruits of his labors are harvested.

It is easy for us to recall the various shapes and sizes of seeds that produce living things, those contained in the fruits and vegetables we eat. Even in God's Word, the reference to seeds is frequent, such as in Isaiah 53:10 "He shall see His seed" as God foretold the coming of His Son that He planted by the Holy Spirit in the Virgin Mary. But when it comes to our relationships with other people and God, what do the seeds look like that will grow to produce strong and healthy spiritual lives filled with the radiant light and love of Christ and with the fellowship of one another? Have you ever thought that a kind word said to someone or a helping hand you give to someone in need may be seeds? Even a smile can be a seed. God has blessed us all with a full compliment of seeds that can promote spiritual growth; all we have to do is start planting them.

In my own workplace, I have discovered many forms and varieties of spiritual seeds. To constantly remind me of my pursuit of righteousness and faithfulness in my spiritual walk, I keep little reminders around me to serve as obvious emblems for others. Some of these *seeds* include:

- The biblically based passwords I use for my computer at work; not only as a reminder to me, but as a witness to others who have access to my computer (such as our information systems staff who trouble shoot and maintain it).
- A little battery-operated clock, nestled between two hands joined together in prayer, which a brother in Christ gave me as a gift.
- My computer screen saver with a continuous scrolling message proclaiming "His plan and His timing."
- A copy of an engineering drawing that I have on my wall at work for a project our company worked on at a site named "Godwantsya Creek" in California (a real place).
- A daily devotional calendar, with a separate scripture for each day.
- An onscreen computer mouse pointer in the shape of a pulsating Bible with a cross on the front.
- A small Ichthus (Christian fish) symbol I added behind my name on my hard hat.
- A copy of the Ten Commandments hanging on my wall.

The list could go on and on. The key to maintaining these physical reminders, in everyone's view, is to maintain the correct level of sensitivity; i.e., to be bold to witness my faith, but not to an extreme. I *am* truly committed to my faith and sometimes I have to control my excitement and enthusiasm. As Jeremiah 20:9 states, "But if I say, 'I will not mention him or speak any more in his name,' his word is in my heart like a fire, a fire shut up in my bones. I am weary of holding it in; indeed, I cannot." Another scripture that comes to mind is the last line of a daily prayer I have adopted: "Let my heart be blameless regarding Your statues, that I may not be ashamed" (Psalm 119:80). I desire to be fully committed to God's ways for me, and to be bold enough to set an example for others. If someone ever asked me what I would be honored to have as an epitaph, it would be: "Ron reflected the face of Christ in his life" (2 Corinthians 3:18).

Unseen Fruit

When we plant God's spiritual seeds, we are faithfully and diligently doing His work, but we are not guaranteed to be present to witness the final fruits. An example of this timing comes from a former co-worker named Don. He was in his late sixties, actually past normal retirement age, when we started our small fellowship group and someone suggested that we invite Don to join us. For several months we gave Don a reminder invitation each week, with no response on his part. One day, without any advanced notice, Don came for the first time, with an expressed curiosity of what we did in our group. Timidly, but with an obvious sense of pride, Don began to share that his son, Don Junior, had been a chaplain in the military and was a pastor of a Church. Don also related that his son was also part of a weekend radio ministry that educated (forewarned) others about various religious cults. Two days after joining us for the first time, Don showed me a newspaper article about Don Jr. and his radio ministry. With the contact information included in the article, I decided to write Don Junior an e-mail message about his father coming to our group. Within a day, Don Junior responded to me, indicating that my note brought tears to his eyes, as he understood his father and mother to be non-believers prior to my message.

For Don, the seed had been planted and now needed to grow. Don came to almost every one of our meetings, more than anyone else, including me. But Don made it clear from the beginning that he just wanted to be there to listen to our discussions, and not be confronted to share his thoughts or give his opinion. Therefore, asking Don to lead us in prayer was not even a consideration, in respect of his wishes. Several years later, Don chose to retire from our business at the age of seventy. Upon his retirement, we presented Don with a new Bible and several other references for his spiritual growth. Although I so much wanted to see Don bloom in his faith, like a flower in spring, I learned that it was not to be, as acceptance of faith would be according to God's plan and timing.

His Timing

Over the last several years, I've found something interesting when I am patient and watch God at work, according to His own plan and His own timing. Shortly after I accepted Christ, I was doing everything I could to live a righteous life like Christ wants for me to grow in my faith. Apparently the change in the way I was living my life became evident to others around me.

A prime example is from a client of mine named Bill. During a business trip together, Bill and I were enjoying a late evening dinner at a hotel restaurant, when Bill asked me about my faith. I spent the short time we had together that evening sharing with him how I came to accept Christ in my life. Bill's interest encouraged me. As time went on, however, Bill never further pursued our discussion. In fact, on several occasions, Bill became very defensive about my faith, from a non-Christian perspective. I even began receiving e-mail messages and stories from Bill on my home computer that were offensive. It got to a point that I would delete his messages before I even opened them.

But God has a plan. A few years later I began receiving e-mail messages from Bill with very uplifting and inspiring stories. I'm not sure why the change in his perspective occurred, but I would make sure to acknowledge him and thank him for the messages. A while later when I met Bill face-to-face after a meeting, I mentioned something to him about the messages he had been sending. He kind of shrugged and said that his wife "has him going to Church again." All I could say to myself was "praise God for all his wondrous works to the children of men, one small step at a time" (Psalm 107:8).

A New Shepherd

With my continuing growth in faith and my experiences in the workplace, I have learned that not only the seeds we plant in non-believers are important. The seeds we plant in the hearts of other believers also become a key element in furthering God's kingdom. The next story is a wonderful example of planting seeds in the heart of believers.

One of my closest brothers in Christ, Jesús, is a truly devoted man of God. Jesús came to Christ during the period of time he worked for our company. Jesús and I have developed a close one-on-one relationship, with our faith as a foundation. We have experienced many life circumstances together. I was honored to be present when he was baptized. When his wife was expecting their first child, Jesús would constantly share with me his feelings as an expectant father. When his daughter was born, I was blessed with the joy of sharing the experience with his family by visiting them while his wife was still in the hospital. Our connection developed further as Jesús shared some of *my* personal life experiences, such as coming to my daughter's wedding, and helping us move them into their new apartment.

With all humility, there were times I felt our relationship paralleled that of Paul and Timothy, with me being called by God to be a mentor to Jesús. We even started a routine of praying together every day before we started our work activities, which was truly a spiritual uplift for both of us. The enthusiasm Jesús displays in his faith is tremendous. That he is bold in His faith is an understatement. He is always there to volunteer his help. In distributing announcements for our meetings, he would provide the extra special touch of spending a moment to talk to others. With a loving heart, Jesús reaches out to others with encouragement and comfort. And as another witnessing tool for a reminder to others, how awesome is it that his name is spelled the same as our Savior's. In every way, Jesús is a true supporter of the workplace ministry.

After several years with our company, Jesús made a decision to leave to pursue opportunities to grow in his career. I know he agonized over this decision for some time, as he shared this process with me from the beginning. Although I didn't look forward to the thought of him not being part of our own workplace ministry, I encouraged him, indicating that it was God's plan for him to shepherd his own flock in a workplace ministry at his new company. As he and I were both excited about this new opportunity to serve the Lord, I advised him to be patient for God's plan to unfold. It took me several years before I felt God's call to start our fellowship group. For Jesús, however, God's plan turned out to be on a fast track. Within one month, Jesús excitedly informed me that he had just had his first fellowship gathering with two other believers at his new workplace. What an awesome God He is!

Jesús is still very close to me. We still make it a point to get together for lunch at least once a month. Then we share our ministry success stories and continue to remind each other that the fruit of our labors is ultimately in God's hands (1 Corinthians 3:6-7).

Faith and Hope

As we plant the seeds of eternal life in the hearts of others, we must continue to be strong willed and determined in our faith. I know this is difficult for me. Sometimes I just want to give up. But I am an individual, and when I start a project, I like to see it finished. Although it may take some time for me to get started and to progress through the process, I ultimately want to see what my labor has produced. Otherwise, why start at all? I think this comes from my desire to set things right, such as in building structures or repairing and strengthening relationships with other people. This may be why I chose to be an engineer in a career where I build things. I have been frequently reminded by supervisors to "plan your work and work your plan" to see ideas to completion.

Although we all hope to be present here on this earth to see the fruits of our labors, we cannot selfishly give up in discouragement and frustration if we don't reach that goal. It may not be God's plan for us. We must continue to persevere and run a good race, regardless of the outcome, as the Apostle Paul wrote and exemplified by his life. In doing so, we must continue to remember and trust that our labors are not in vain, for God has a plan: "Faith is the substance of things hoped for, the evidence of things not seen" (Hebrews 11:1). How true this is in the overall scheme of our universe.

7

A FINE LINE

When I was fifteen years old, my father, who was employed by a hi-tech business as an electrical engineer, decided to purchase a small eighty-acre farm to work in his spare time. Some of his business associates had done the same thing, so he jumped on the bandwagon and followed their lead. As a result, we moved to a rural setting where I was exposed to some of the aspects of farm life I might not otherwise have experienced. When one paints a picture in his mind of a farm, the one thing that would probably be included is fences that surround the fields and pastures. Boy, do I know of fences. I distinctly remember helping to build and repair many fences, most of which were the permanent type with wood posts set in the ground and barbed wire tightly strung between them at three or four levels.

Another type of fence that many people are not as familiar with is an electric fence. Such a fence temporarily subdivides permanently fenced areas to contain livestock for grazing and other purposes. This type of fence consists of a single small bare wire, probably the diameter of a piece of uncooked thin spaghetti. The wire stretches between electrical insulators attached to metal rods that can be easily pushed or pounded into the ground. For best results, the wire is normally installed about two to three feet above the ground. Attached at some point along the fence is an insulated wire that connects a pulsating electrical power supply, which operates at the same voltage as a regular household electrical outlet. Although difficult to spot unless close to it, the primary intent of this type of fence is to be an effective containment, yet be temporary and easily moved around and reconfigured as necessary. It *was* very effective, since I was shocked on several occasions when I didn't pay close attention to its location and brushed up against it.

I mention my farming experience because it forms a tangible analogy to what workers experience in the workplace. The *fine line*, as I refer to it, is what we face as acceptable and unacceptable behavior and conduct in our workplace (our fields). When we enter into the workplace environment, we are usually presented with a list of written rules that we are expected to follow. The written rules may include a definition of our working hours, use of company equipment and supplies, prohibition of drugs and alcohol, codes of conduct, etc. The unwritten rules, however, are those fine lines that usually are left open to interpretation. Just like an electric fence, these fine lines are difficult to define or see. They can provide us with a sudden jolt if we are confronted with crossing the line, but surprisingly enough, they are not permanent or immovable. As Christians in the workplace, it is our calling to be bold in sharing our faith, with the challenge to nudge that fine line, little by little, in the name of Christ. My own daily motivation to making a difference in being bold for Christ is captured in the last line of my daily prayer, "May my heart be blameless according to Your statutes, that I may not be ashamed" (Psalm 119:80).

How Did We Get Here?

As an American, it is interesting and yet disheartening to recall our history and what led to the separation of faith from the normal accepted culture in the secular workplace. At the time the pilgrims settled in Massachusetts, the reason many people left England was to seek the freedom to worship according to their own beliefs. Many of those who made the journey to this new land were of varying Christian faiths, but they shared the common thread of a desire for freedom to worship God in their own way. Thus, it is accurate to say that our country was founded on faith in God.

Today, as we enter into the twenty-first century, more than ever we see non-believers crying "foul" when anyone perceives some life circumstance violating their rights under the First Amendment to the United States Constitution. Although this amendment dictates a separation of Church and State by forbidding the endorsement of any specific religion, it also guarantees the freedom to everyone to worship according to their own beliefs. Over the past two centuries, especially in the latter part of the 1900's, application of the First Amendment has become progressively biased against any visible display of religious beliefs. Examples range from not being allowed to publicly pray before a high school football game, to a move by an individual to remove the reference to God in the *Pledge of Allegiance*. It wouldn't be surprising if someone took on the cause to remove references to God on most of our currency. To conform to this, the governmental workplace has been careful to maintain a clear position on this separation of Church and State, all the way from the federal government to the local government. The private workplace has been quick to follow suit, as many of them have direct business relationships with the government. As a result, in the majority of workplaces, even many of those who profess to be Christian based businesses, there is a stigma placed on any conduct that has any semblance of religion. Such an environment has conditioned Christians to keep silent about faith, otherwise they may be made an example of misconduct or even be ostracized. It is clearly evident that the evil one is busy, and from a quick glance, seems to be winning in these times. But we know better. We can do something about him and we will be the winners in the end.

<u>What Can We Do?</u>

There is much we can do, and God will be with us to guide us every step of the way. We *must* put our trust in Him. The one thing we cannot do is *do nothing*. To overcome the current perceptions and limitations the workplace places on us, we must be bold. This process will definitely require many of us to step out of our comfort zone. Jesus, Himself, told us so when he powerfully warned (and challenged) His disciples:

> If the world hates you, keep in mind that it hated me first. If you belonged to the world, it would love you as its own. As it is, you do not belong to the world, but I have chosen you out of the world. That is why the world hates you. Remember the words I spoke to you: 'No servant is greater than his master.' If they persecuted me, they will persecute you also. If they obeyed my teaching, they will obey yours also. They will treat you this way because of my name, for they do not know the One who sent me. If I had come and spoken to them, they would not be guilty of sin. Now, however, they have no excuse for their sin. He who hates me hates my Father as well. If I had not done among them what no one else did, they would not be guilty of sin. But now they have seen these miracles, and yet they have hated both me and my Father. But this is to fulfill what is written in their Law: 'They hated me without reason' (John 15:18-25).

Jesus continues by telling His disciples how they will be ostracized and physically harmed, even facing death. But to give in to the ways of the world is to reject Jesus.

When we first started our fellowship group, it wasn't long before we were tested in a similar way. A little over a month after we first began meeting, my supervisor, who joined in our group, was approached by someone who took issue with what we were doing. The individual, who remained unidentified to us, apparently told my supervisor something to the effect that our group meeting shouldn't be going on here, and you, Mr. Supervisor, shouldn't be a part of it. The result of this complaint could have been that we just give up meeting all together. But determined to follow what Jesus had

30

commanded us, we worked with our human resources director and developed a mutual compromise. We would make sure we weren't intentionally or unintentionally making a visual display of our study materials (e.g. the Bible) as we went to/from our meeting place, we would keep the room door shut during our time together, and we would strictly adhere to our meeting duration (which we should do anyway to respect company guidelines). Whether or not this compromise satisfied the individual who complained isn't apparent, but we have not had a formal issue made since that time. Consequently, with respect and sensitivity to others, we have referred to our group as The Lunch Group, with no reference to our purpose. Our word of mouth discretely ministering to others provides all the advertising we need for God to put those in our path who need to know Christ.

The Information Technology Line

The information age, with computer systems and e-mail communication, has opened up a vast new way of reaching others for Christ. In our workplace ministry, we have tested the corporate acceptance of using e-mail communications for this purpose. There are times when use of company computers and e-mail messaging for non-business purposes can cross over the line of acceptable conduct. When this occurs, the company's response is to send out a global corporate message to remind all users of the accepted policies. Any continuance of unacceptable usage would be followed with other enforcement action, although the initial reminder is usually enough to get the point across.

When we first started our fellowship group, we used the company e-mail system to issue weekly reminders of our meetings, without much thought to the correctness of doing so. Although we only sent the messages to those we knew would be interested in receiving them, and after several corporate reminders of unacceptable e-mail system usage (prompted by other staff regarding unrelated subject matter), we soon realized that this approach was not appropriate. Instead, we elected to hand distribute written reminders, which in itself was an improvement in ministry by having one-on-one, face-to-face personal contact with others in our office. There will be those rare times, however, when we do use the e-mail system for sharing circumstances requesting prayer and for sharing a special story or thought for inspiration and encouragement in our faith walk. When we do author such messages, we are sensitive even to the words we use, such as frequently substituting "thoughts" for "prayer," and referring to He, Him, or His in lieu of outwardly referring to God, Jesus, or our Lord. There is no intent of trying to hide our faith, but just to use the system to its fullest acceptable limits while testing the *fine line*.

Another recent encouraging development in the expansion of this ministry involves a participant in one of our other corporate offices, who has established a similar Christian fellowship group and started a weekly inspirational e-mail message called *ABC Light* (ABC being an alias of our company name, for the purpose of anonymity). Some may relate the word *light* to "less filling" as some food and beverage advertising promotes, but it is an expression of removing the darkness we have in this world and filling it with the light of Christ. The author of this periodic inspirational message provided me with the following note regarding his work:

> I would be honored to have you include [in this book] the work the spirit is doing through (a.k.a.) *ABC Light. ABC Light* started out of some conversations with colleagues on how we get so much junk but very little encouragement in our e-mail. Ideas for the first *Lights* grew out of an office Bible study that we used to hold. From there it really took on a life of its own; 1) in terms of the ideas coming out of feedback from others, books I had read on faith in the workplace, and my own devotions/personal reflections; 2) a rapidly growing list of voluntary recipients that adds one or two new members each week. The *Light* is now sent to a large internal list of employees from top management to new staff. The external list is equally diverse, ranging from large utility CEO's to my mom. Each message appears to touch different people in different ways and it has become a journal for my own faith journey. I don't know where this journey is headed but I am enjoying the trip.

Above all, as God would have us do, we are ever conscious of the respect we must have for the corporate principals in the workplace, yet we must continue to walk the fine line as God directs us in His work.

Living Examples

In this world of so many lost souls, it brings great joy to my heart to see examples of people who are bold enough to witness their faith, who put their complete trust in God and are not afraid to step over any fine lines the world has drawn. These examples emerge from the common man who may only be known to his family and local community to personalities in the media who the whole world knows. They are everywhere if we only look closely.

An example of a common man is a friend of mine named Mitch. Mitch and I became friends through a mutual business contact within the organization where he works. Several years ago, Mitch accepted Christ as his Savior. As a law enforcement officer, Mitch has many face-to-face encounters with the full variety of individuals who drive the roadways. He has shared that it becomes a real test of his faith to deal with the nasty words and actions of some individuals as he performs his duty delivering warnings and citations for traffic infractions. Nevertheless, Mitch continues to be strengthened by his faith during these times and uses opportunities to be like Jesus to those who may not even know Him. If there is ever a doubt in Mitch's mind of his vocational calling, Romans 13:1 is his support: "Everyone must submit himself to the governing authorities, for there is no authority except that which God has established."

Another example is my brother-in-Christ, Jesús, the new shepherd that I spoke of earlier. Within a year of his entrance into his new company, Jesús was faced with another hurdle that he had to confront head on, that of his corporation tightening its policy on religious freedom. In a letter to his management, Jesús wrote:

> I appreciate your visit to [our] office and your presentation on a positive environment in the workplace. Much of the information was useful and helpful. Yet, I am writing this letter to express disagreement on a [company] policy that in my opinion appears to have been hastily made and without thorough consideration of the potential adverse impacts it may have to a 'positive work environment.' The policy in question is the elimination of prayer or religious based fellowship in [the company's] conference rooms.
>
> A 'positive work environment' can be manifested in many ways. Eliminating the potential for harassment is certainly beneficial. Another way to create a positive environment is to acknowledge that there is a spiritual component to many employees, including myself. Denying the use of available meeting space during non-business hours discourages the faith-filled employee. It is a blanket elimination of spirituality for all religions. For those employees that depend on God as a source of hope, guidance, and strength daily, the elimination of conference rooms for religious gatherings does not lead to a positive environment.
>
> Personally, I live for Jesus the Christ and everything I do is in an attempt to glorify him. I do not actively proselytize at work because I understand some find it offensive. Yet many know what I believe in and several employees ask for prayers during times of need. More recently, one approached me regarding prayer for a parent in ill health.

After prayer, a tearful thank you was his reply as he rushed to get to his father's side. This is a true and sincere example of a 'positive work environment.' I was with a different employer during the attacks of 9/11. Immediately afterwards there was a conference room available for prayer during that frightful time. Truly, I state, there was much gratitude towards management for that gesture and they were rightfully appreciated.

Now [the company] has a large contract to rebuild the infrastructure in Iraq. Some from [our] office have already left and others from throughout the nation will soon follow. As you most certainly know, they are in a precarious situation. In my humble opinion, they need prayer both for themselves and the family members they leave behind. Because of the subdued excitement of this opportunity, I encourage [the company] to overturn this policy and encourage a 'positive work environment' by acknowledging the faith-filled employee and making conference rooms available to prayer.

Although there may be different approaches and sensitivity levels in dealing with such situations, there is no doubt about the boldness of Jesús in carrying his message to those who could change the policy. As the full story became known, a single incident in Jesús' company had caused this fallout, followed by the corporation overreacting with this global dictate. When the dust settled, Jesús received reassurance from company representatives that a reasonable level of faith-based activity would be tolerated, a.k.a. the *fine line*.

There are probably some Christian media personalities who, to different degrees, are bold to witness their faith. One that comes to mind is Kirk Cameron from the television show "Growing Pains." Furthermore, Kirk portrayed Buck Williams in the movie from the novel series "Left Behind." Towards the later years of Kirk's role in "Growing Pains," he accepted Christ as his Savior. As others in the cast remember, Kirk, previously the "jokester" with a carefree and playful attitude, had become more serious and mature in his attitude. In their eyes, this complete change in Kirk's character (repentance) showed that he had become withdrawn. The truth was that Kirk was now focusing on living his life as God wanted by following Jesus Christ. Kirk's change dramatically influenced the show, as Kirk took issue with those parts of the scripts that did not reflect a wholesome and Christian lifestyle. He was insistent enough in his beliefs that the show's producers had to comply with his wishes in order to continue the series with Kirk as part of the cast. What a testimony his example provides for maintaining and stepping over the fine line the world sets before us.

A day after the Columbia Space Shuttle tragedy in January 2003, I felt an overwhelming prompting of the Holy Spirit to write the following about a man the whole world knows:

> One of the real challenges we face as Christians in the workplace is dealing with the *fine line*. What is the *fine line*? It is the unwritten or unspoken limits that attempt to define what is acceptable conduct, as judged by others (on this earth) for whom and with whom we work. It's like playing a game without really knowing the rules. You have to play and test the limits of behavior to discover what the rules are.
>
> To live our lives in the workplace by reflecting the face of Christ to others, we will definitely run into obstacles. If our conduct crosses the line, we may be confronted, or even held accountable for our actions. The real test of our faith and commitment to Christ is what we do at these times. Do we back off, turn around, and walk away, or do we become more determined to push the limit to a new level that is compromisingly acceptable for everyone? *All* of us, yes every one of us, has been called by God to be bold in our faith, to live our lives in Christ, and to bring others to know Him. When our lives are complete on this earth, and we ultimately come before Him to be judged for our final and eternal reward, it is not enough just to be a good person, believing in Him and accepting His Son as our Lord and Savior. We will be judged on what we have done with the gifts He has given us. So much of God's Word tells us this. Therefore, what are *you* doing now to push the line?
>
> Regardless of what you think about his performance in office, or what your political affiliation is, we are indeed truly blessed by God to have a President like George W. Bush. His public witnessing of his faith *is* definitely pushing the line and setting an example, in the highest level workplace, in the nation. It is openly known that the president has a daily Bible study with his staff. President Bush has also been deliberate in integrating his faith and references to God in many of his public statements, much to the chagrin of his speechwriters and staunch advocates of the First Amendment. In fact, two days after his State of the Union Address on January 28, 2003, the *USA Today* newspaper carried an article entitled "Bush's Agenda Walks the Church-state Line," which highlighted many of his references to God and his faith in his message. Then four days

later with the Columbia space shuttle tragedy on February 1, 2003, President Bush's first public statement to the nation referenced Isaiah 40:26 and the coming home (to be with God) of the astronauts.

In these times, there is a real sense of urgency that God is trying to instill in each of us (knock, knock, anyone home in there?). Eighteen months ago we witnessed the 9/11 tragedy. The Columbia tragedy has again reminded us how our lives on this earth can end in an instant. Soon we may become witnesses to a much larger tragedy if war begins in the Middle East. The urgency is for each of us to get ourselves right with God *now* by witnessing others. No matter where you are on the hierarchy of an organizational chart in the workplace (as exemplified by President Bush), *every one* of us must push ourselves to be bold, and without hesitation, push the *fine line* to bring others to Christ.

What more can I say? We are called to be bold and to witness our faith. Not unlike the workplace where those who know Christ are cautiously accepted, Jesus was in a similar situation with the woman at the well in Samaria (John 4). As this example demonstrates, the faithfulness and boldness of believers must continue to spread the good news, even after they have been confronted and told to stop doing so. Luke best describes this in Acts 16:35-40, as the Apostle Paul provides a clear and determined persistence to continue delivering the gospel. I urge you to take time to read and reflect on this passage.

8
OUTSIDE THE
WALLS

With any endeavor on which we truly focus, we may find ourselves becoming so self absorbed and introspective that we forget to *think outside the box* (a phrase that has become overused, but is appropriate here). In any ministry of faith, whether in the Church, community, or mission field, we need to step back from time to time to see where we are, where we are going, and what the needs of others are. Two areas of ministry that have similar needs in reaching outside their walls are the Church and the workplace.

Church Missions

Over the past years that I have pursued God's calling to this fine line ministry, I have come to understand that this is not intended to be an alternative or replacement for Church, but a mission field of the Church. On more than one occasion, I have witnessed a non-believer come to our fellowship group seeking to learn more about the Christian faith, who said that he or she was more comfortable coming into a meeting room with those one knows and works with than entering the doors of a Church as a total stranger. It's unfortunate some people feel this way, but after all isn't reaching outside the walls of the Church building and body to touch the lives of others and bring them to Christ what Church missions are all about?

Here is where the commitment of Church ministries gets clouded, and from my own perspective, I see that a reawakening needs to occur. On numerous occasions, I have approached the ministry staff of different Churches to share what God is doing in the workplace and its potential for bringing others to Christ. What's discouraging is that in each case, there has been a disinterested attitude. Although none of the ministry staffs took issue with what I was involved in, they essentially ignored any overtures I made to get the Church involved.

At one Church, I sponsored a booth at its ministry fair to promote the workplace ministry. There was some interest from those who toured the fair, but the Church ministry staff did not catch on to the idea. At another Church I personally met with ministry staff for one-on-one discussions and even offered to speak to groups within the Church, but no follow-up response or interest on their part followed. I even suggested this ministry in a questionnaire that the Church circulated requesting ideas for new ministries, again with no response.

Initially, these failed attempts to further God's kingdom through the Church brought on feelings of hurt, frustration, and even rejection. I would try to rationalize why this was happening (or not happening). I thought that some of the reasons why the Church might be reluctant to get involved in this type of ministry *(and my own corresponding rationale)* are:

- The association of their Church (by name) or its members with activities in the workplace could lead to negative image perceptions by employers. *(The Church is not intended to be a direct sponsor of its members in the workplace, only to encourage them to follow God's direction.)*
- The workplace ministry, as an outreach mission, is not part of their Church plans (vision or budget). *(The Church is needed to provide a place to gather workers from within to be trained and encouraged to be part of this ministry, so each trained person can implement the fine line ministry in their own workplace. There are no real financial needs of this ministry from the Church, only willing workers to gather the plentiful harvest.)*
- Many of the Church ministry staff may be far removed from or unfamiliar with the real secular workplace culture on a day-to-day basis. *(This can be overcome in time and with further dialog designed to sensitize Church ministry staff to the secular workplace world condition.)*
- I am viewed as not having received any formal theological training to effectively lead a ministry. *(God has prepared me to lead this ministry and continues to guide me as I grow in my faith.)*

After many attempts to enter the Church body with this ministry, I finally began to sense God's presence in dealing with my feelings. I now realize that all I need to do, as with anything, is to put my trust in God to achieve His will. It is truly His plan, according to His timing. By surrendering all things to Him in furthering this ministry, the stumbling block of second guessing myself has been removed. I now have a sense of peace, joy, and anticipation as He continues to reveal His plan to me. God continues to place opportunities before me within the Church where I can *plant seeds* by following up with people on a one-on-one basis as I hear of their own trials in the workplace.

<u>Workplace Outreach</u>

What has been really encouraging to me is that Christian fellowship in the workplace, similar to the Church, has its own opportunities to go outside beyond the walls. God presents many of these opportunities to us without any of our own worldly planning. It can be as simple as a co-worker exploring his or her faith by talking with other Christians in the workplace, and then taking the thoughts of these discussions home to share further with family and friends. It's similar to catching an illness such as the common cold from someone at work. Then, through the natural course of living, it is taken home where others in the family catch it. So, too, is the spreading of the good news with a much better result of healing rather than illness.

A brother-in-Christ in our workplace named Richard is very active in his large Church. He truly has a servant's heart. Several times a year this Church puts on a spectacular production to convey God's message to the world. Richard and his family are always intimately involved. One such time is at Christmas. Each year Richard diligently spreads the word within our office about this production to encourage others to attend. I have attended these presentations myself and come away with a satisfying feeling of the presence of the Holy Spirit as the gospel is delivered to many lost souls.

One such *lost* person is another co-worker named Lonnie. I met Lonnie several years ago when he joined our firm as the head of our office CAD (Computer Aided Drafting) group. I wasn't really sure where he was in his spiritual walk because nothing was clearly evident on the surface. A short while after Lonnie had been with us, the Christmas season approached. Richard began promoting their Church Christmas production and our workplace fellowship group decided to get several of us together to go to the program. We made it an extended Saturday evening by having dinner at a local restaurant and going on to Richard's Church. To my excitement, Lonnie and his wife decided to join our group for this night of fellowship. The next Monday, Lonnie shared with several of us how the message really touched his heart. It was very clear that the seed to the heart of Jesus had been planted in Lonnie.

Only a few months later, as a Promise Keepers conference in our area was fast approaching, I suggested to the men in our workplace fellowship group the idea of attending it together. I hadn't really heard much from Lonnie about how his walk in faith had progressed since the Christmas program, so I asked him if he would be interested in going to Promise Keepers with our group. I was so pleased that, without any hesitation, Lonnie agreed to come. As the day to attend the conference approached, all the other men dropped out for various reasons, all except Lonnie. The time Lonnie and I spent together, one-on-one, was truly God's plan. Although it was originally meant to be another fellowship gathering outside the workplace walls, it became God's time to further nurture Lonnie's spiritual growth. There is much more to Lonnie's remarkable story, which I will share later. This story illustrates well how workplace ministry can extend beyond its own walls.

Another way to extend our Christian fellowship beyond the workplace walls is to share in the life events of others. My friend Jesús, who became the shepherd of a new flock when he went to work for another company, comes to mind again. Before he left our company, I had the privilege to be present at his own Church at the time of his baptism. Not only was this holy time what it was meant to be, but also afterwards it provided the opportunity to make a connection to our workplace as Jesús introduced me to others in his Church as a Christian from his fellowship group at work. Sharing in God's plan is such an *awesome* experience. We could never plan such things ourselves, even if we tried for an entire lifetime on this earth.

Extended Workplaces

If we think outside the walls, the possibilities are limitless. Let's not just think of only our own workplace fellowship opportunities, but of those extended places where we may work. As a consulting engineer, I serve and work with our company clients many times in their own offices. In one exceptional case, we had been afforded the use of dedicated office space in a client's own workplace since we interface with their staff on such a frequent basis. This situation provided the opportunity to get to know many of their staff on a more personal level. Such casual conversation over time revealed those of faith and another field to harvest.

Further in distance from our own office are our other corporate offices. Over the past few years, work sharing between offices has presented opportunities to better know staff in their workplaces, again revealing those of faith and more fields to harvest. Through encouragement and prayer, several of these offices have formed their own Christian fellowship groups. We continue to remain in constant touch to learn from and encourage one another. A staff member of one of these offices authors the *ABC Light* spiritual message referenced earlier in Chapter 7, which now has a readership beyond the workplace walls.

Other Workplaces

There are many other workplaces (which are not associated with our own workplace activities) where we can touch the lives of others. Such places are those that provide us various services in our personal lives. I remember several years ago when I was being treated for a detached retina in my left eye.

I had already undergone two surgeries to repair the retina the first time, when the retina detached again. As I was in the hospital for another surgery, I took with me the most current novel in the *"Left Behind"* series to read while I waited for the procedure to begin. Although I never gave it a thought, the book series based on "Revelation," the last book in the Bible, spurred some comments and discussions with the hospital attending staff both before and after the operation.

As I was being prepped for the surgery during which I would remain conscious, I felt an overwhelming prompting of the Holy Spirit as I asked the surgeon if I could pray with and for the operating staff prior to the procedure. I think he was a little taken aback by such a request, but he agreed. I was wheeled into the operating room and went through the extensive and meticulous ordeal that literally tied me down on the table, while the area around my eye where the surgeon would perform his skilled work was properly cleansed and prepared. Then, hovering over me with a surgical instrument in his hand, the surgeon said, "Okay, we're ready for you," meaning it was now time for me to pray. As I slowly and deliberately lifted my circumstances up to the Lord as spoken prayer, including prayer for the surgeon and the attending staff, I could only imagine what they all thought. My purpose for prayer was a sincere petition to God, but I really wonder how those present might recall this petition in later discussion among themselves. What an outreach ministry opportunity.

There have been times when I have thought that as a workplace fellowship group we should do something more together outside the walls, such as serving in a community outreach program. One co-worker suggested that we assist in a local ministry that mentored to children and youth who had only one parent, usually a mother without the father figure. It was a little disheartening to me that although there was some initial enthusiasm about this idea, and one of our group members checked into it further, nothing materialized. It was not that this was a bad idea or wouldn't be a good idea for another workplace fellowship group to pursue, but it was apparently not God's plan for us. My key mistake was making it *my* idea, not His. So much can and will be accomplished through His plan, not ours. What I have shared here is only a sampling of the glorious work in which we can be a part of and accomplish only through Him.

9

THE HARVEST

R emember the earlier story about the seed-planting project back in grade school? Well, after we planted, the hardest part was yet to come because of our impatience in waiting for something to happen. We knew what the final outcome should look like, as depicted by a picture on the seed package. Several times the first day and daily after that, we would go to the window ledge to check the progress of our labors. Some watered their mini-garden so much that it looked like a swamp; I wondered if seeds could drown. Others, who were either forgetful or visibly disinterested in this project, let their gardens dry up to the point that they developed open cracks like an arid desert. In the end, those of us who faithfully cared for and nurtured our plants, and saw the fruits of our labors with beautiful budding flowers that turned into something that was nourishing to eat, although most kids didn't agree since they didn't like vegetables.

Most of us forget or take for granted the sweat and labor required to produce all the good things God provides for us. Day after day and year after year, farmers commit their lives to working the good earth, planting, and harvesting. God looks over them to provide fertile soil, good weather, and seeds to plant. Through *their* toil, *we* are the benefactors of God's goodness. These truly devoted servants continue to work hard and are persistent in the task to gather in the harvest.

If God wants for us to gather the harvest, then why does He not make it much easier for us to do so? It goes back to the fall of man at the time of Adam and Eve, when God said to Adam:

> Cursed is the ground for your sake; in toil you shall eat of
> it all the days of your life. Both thorns and thistles it shall
> bring forth for you. And you shall eat the herb of the field.
> In the sweat of your face you shall eat bread till you return
> to the ground, for out of it you were taken; for dust you are,
> and to dust your shall return (Genesis 3:17-19).

Like the farmer, we are all called to work the fields that have been planted by the spirit as the Gospel of Matthew states, "The harvest is plentiful, but the labors are few. Ask the Lord of the harvest, therefore, to send out workers into the harvest field" (Matthew 9:37-38). This task is not easy, but God's Word to us is rich with His calling for us to be the workers. Once we have accepted Jesus Christ into our hearts as our Lord and Savior, we are to serve and not to be served. At the end of time as we stand before God to be judged, He will not be looking for where we are in our spiritual walk, but what we have done for others. Leading others to know Christ by bringing in the spiritual harvest is what our lives should emphasize. "But the seed on good soil stands for those with a noble and good heart, who hear the word, return it, and by preserving produce a crop" (Luke 8:15). As Jesus' workers, we need to plant His fields.

As workers in the spiritual fields, each of us may perform different tasks at different times. Sometimes we will be called to plant. Other times we will be called to cultivate and nurture. And if we are truly blessed by God, we may have the opportunity to experience the time of harvest. Although there is not a guarantee that we will witness the gathering of lost souls, it is an indescribable experience when it happens.

After several years of planting seeds in the workplace, I began selfishly feeling the need to see the fruits of my labors. Realizing there are not any guarantees and putting aside my selfishness reluctantly and obediently, I became resolved not to expect a chance to witness the salvation of another. Serving the Lord is my own reward. I knew if I would ever experience someone's conversion, it was to be according to God's own plan and in His own timing as Jeremiah 29:11 indicates. What I did not know was that God's reward for my faithfulness was about to be revealed.

As my co-worker, Lonnie, began his walk of faith, he had just one toe in the water. When I became more acquainted with Lonnie, I discovered that he had once been a servant of God as a pastor at several different Churches. As he related to me, however, he left being a pastor by his own convictions of faith after being divorced. Shortly after this time he began suffering the symptoms of post-polio, being afflicted with polio earlier in life. This condition has confined Lonnie to a wheelchair for most tasks. Between this condition and several other family health issues, Lonnie had really slipped away from his relationship with the Lord. He once told me he knew where he should be in his faith (pointing to his head), but it wasn't here (pointing to his heart).

I talked to Lonnie many times about his faith. Since Lonnie was theologically trained and very well versed in biblical teaching, I felt like a student trying to teach the teacher. I didn't give up though, and I really felt the presence of the Holy Spirit working through me with the helpful words I spoke to Lonnie at the right times. He continued to slip further and further away, until one weekend when he received more bad news about the health of another family member. This was his turning point.

Lonnie knew in his heart that it was time to give all things up to the hands of the Lord. Following up on previous invitations I had given Lonnie to attend Church with me, he tried contacting me to attend Church together that Sunday. Failing to make contact, however, Lonnie went to another Church where God *did* speak to his heart. Lonnie attended Church with me the following two Sundays, where God so spoke to his heart that I think he was left stunned. At our next fellowship lunch at work, he proceeded to stun all of us by making a public confession. Lonnie had turned the corner and was giving his life back to Christ. This fruit was indeed being harvested.

Lonnie's conversion was miraculous as his following e-mail (sent to lift up my spirits when I felt spent in my ministry efforts) conveys:

> I recently heard about a man who had left the ministry and had been out of close fellowship with the Lord for a long time. Another Christian, with a humble heart, gently witnessed to him on several occasions over an eighteen-month period, encouraging him to renew his walk with Christ.
>
> To make a long and beautiful story short, as a result of this witnessing and the leading of the Holy Spirit, this ex-pastor renewed his commitment to Christ and began teaching a Sunday school class. Every week he fostered growth in his class members and had seen their spiritual walk. In addition, the ex-pastor's wife, as a result of her husband's renewed commitment, also accepted Christ and changed paths from heading to hell to heading to heaven. Now she provides transportation to a ninety-year-old blind lady, taking her to Church services as well as Church related social functions. Just a few days ago, the blind lady talked to some people about her newfound friend, a converted Catholic, and ended up explaining to them that God can work in anybody's life.
>
> All of this harvesting occurred because one of God's children faithfully passed out tracts, maintained his witness, and allowed the Holy Spirit to work through him.

10

A Vision

When I think of the word *vision* in a worldly sense, I would define it as "planning through wisdom." As humans with the ability to think and reason, we want to set goals and make plans to achieve them. Webster's dictionary defines *vision* as: "(1) mode of seeing or conceiving, (2) unusual discernment or foresight." In a Godly manner, however, it means that God is revealing Himself to us through prayer and a close relationship with Him. The Bible relates to us many situations where God has revealed to others the path He wishes them to pursue, but the final goal is for only Him to know. In Isaiah 53, God reveals to Isaiah and to His people the coming of the Messiah, which would occur over seven centuries later. Similarly, in the book of Revelation, John receives the vision from God of the second coming of Jesus Christ, which is also yet to come in His time. As true and faithful servants of the Lord, we must put our full trust in Him to guide us and use us in His ultimate plan.

Before and even after accepting Christ into my life, the thought of people receiving one or more visions from God was foreign to me. Yes, I believed that visions truly happened to people, but I thought they were for those who were specially anointed by God for some divine and holy purpose. I would never have believed that I would be one to receive a vision from God. I can't say that I was ever in a mental or psychological state referred to as a *trance*, where one is in "a state of partly suspended animation or inability to function,"[6] but I do know God has spoken to me.

Although I can't exactly remember when it happened, after being involved in this workplace ministry for one or two years, I began to consciously be aware of thoughts coming to mind of the potential outreach the ministry could (or would) have. At first, as my human side prevailed, I thought these were great ideas. I found myself spending time trying to figure out how and when to implement these ideas. Some of them were of such large proportions, however, that I couldn't even imagine where to begin. I think this immensity of scale was what brought me back to my senses. These were not my ideas. These were actually visions of the future that God was revealing to me. In one way, these glimpses gave me comfort knowing that it was not to be by my own devices or schedule, but by His plan and in His time. Although I felt anxious to see this ministry become reality, I shortly realized that according to His timing, I might not be around to witness it. With this perspective, I realized that I am a part of His work for His purpose, and I do rejoice in this opportunity. I guess that may be how John felt when he authored "Revelation."

Workplace Fellowship Groups

One of the first plans I feel God has in store for this ministry is the expansion of workplace fellowship groups, not only in my own company, but also throughout other workplaces in this nation and the world. On a very small scale, I have already experienced the creation of several fellowship groups in the offices of my own nationwide company as well as some other companies (some original fellowship members have left our company and started groups in their new companies.) I'm sure this workplace fellowship is not something new. There are undoubtedly other such Christian fellowships groups in workplaces around the country and other parts of the world. But without a network connection to identify and gather these groups together for one common goal of sharing and encouragement, it is difficult to imagine the level of involvement at this time.

God has laid on my heart the creation of a global workplace ministry. To start with, He has determined that it shall be called the Workplace Christian Fellowship Ministry (WCFM). I know for a time I tried to come up with what to call this ministry, but regardless of my ideas, this title kept reoccurring in my mind. Therefore, I trusted in His plan. In February 2004, WCFM officially became a recorded non-profit ministry in the State of Florida. The WCFM mission statement captures the essence of this ministry: "To encourage, develop, and support Christian fellowship in the workplace, which promotes a positive environment for believers to walk and grow in their faith following Jesus Christ, while honoring their workplace obligations and duties." Regardless of what this ministry is called, the primary purpose, God's purpose, is to create a wave of spiritual awakening where the drought of spirituality has become severe. A unity of the spirit in the workplace definitely needs to be established. Through the many worldly events happening today, I feel a sense of urgency in God's plan for getting this organization implemented.

In addition to this book and the exposure it may have, our electronic communication age can catapult this ministry into worldwide view. A WCFM Web site will be created which will clearly communicate the mission of this ministry. It needs to be a place of sharing and education for dealing with the *fine line* obstacles that will be encountered in any workplace. It should also provide an interactive dialog that will encourage others to boldly witness their faith in the workplace and provide feedback of issues where assistance and direction may be required. United as one body in Christ, we can shake up the world. All that is needed is a sincere commitment from those who can support this ministry with their time and talents.

Gather 'Round

In the mid-1990's, when I was exposed to the activities in which my daughter Abby was involved as part of her Church youth group, I was introduced to a yearly event that is uplifting and encouraging and inspired another idea for workplace fellowship. The time of this yearly event is usually in September. The location is at public schools all across the nation. The event or gathering is called "See You at the Pole." For those people unfamiliar with this gathering, it is basically a call to prayer for all school students who wish to participate. I have even heard of teachers joining the group. Students and faculty taking part usually meet early in the morning at the flagpole in front of their school building before school starts. Holding hands, they form a ring around the pole and begin to pray for whatever their hearts wish to express and lift up to the Lord.

To date, I am unaware of any situations where praying in front of schools has been prohibited. Since these schools are public institutions administered by governmental bodies, such religious gatherings are especially prone to come under attack on the basis of separation of Church and State.[7] In fact, many students, and again even some faculty, have continued this prayer at the pole on a more frequent basis during the school year. The fearful reality is that it will probably only be a matter of time until this practice comes under fire from the secular world.

To help further strengthen our resolve for fellowship in the workplace, and to allow the parents of these children to get involved in the same bold witness, God has laid a vision on my heart to follow the lead of these children and have co-workers gather together in our workplace locations. The plan would simply entail the promotion of people in all workplace environments to come together to pray on the same day each year that these children gather together around the flagpole at their schools. Since workplaces may not have a flagpole or even a building (such as construction workers or other mobile vocations), the primary emphasis would be to gather around wherever the situation permits.

For several years as I was inspired by this idea, the time in September of each year came and went. The first year was only one week after the 9-11 tragedy, so I felt it was not the opportune time (my thinking again, not God's). The following year came and went so quickly that I again missed the chance to prepare in advance for this opportunity. Leading into the third annual opportunity, I again was not prepared, but God was. He lit the spark that would overcome my human inaction. It came as He touched the life of another believer in my workplace.

Lew was a man I didn't have a chance to get to know too well. He was one whom I distributed my weekly fellowship meeting reminders to each week at work, but since he was frequently out of the office on business, our paths rarely crossed. One day in September 2003, Lew came to my office wanting to talk to me. It was obvious he was excited about something and needed to share it with me. It was a few days before the annual "See You at the Pole" prayer gathering. Lew told me that he had been at his Church where one of his children attended a youth group gathering. They were distributing wristbands, like the WWJD ones, which spelled out "See You at the Pole," to promote the next day's prayer gatherings at schools. In the course of being there, Lew was also given one of the bands. The day before the prayer gathering, Lew participated in a business meeting with one of his clients when someone asked him about the wristband he was wearing. To Lew's surprise, after he explained the purpose of the wristband, his client suggested that they, too, gather around their office flagpole the next morning to pray. God's gentle nudging had begun.

After relating this exciting and encouraging news to me, I asked Lew if he would please return the next day to let me know how this workplace prayer gathering went. As Lew left my office, I could feel the largest grin spread across my face as I turned to the Father in prayer and praise, knowing it was all happening according to His plan and His timing. The next day Lew returned to my office to share the morning's events: close to twenty of these workplace individuals gathered in public prayer, some of them passionately led by the spirit. Shortly afterwards, I wrote a message to Lew, reminding him that this gathering was only the beginning—a possible future expansion of this prayer occasion to other workplaces could occur. Also, it presented a God-given workplace with a flock of believers that Lew could gather together and shepherd. Only time according to God's own plan will reveal where this ministry may lead.

A Church Mission

Although I have personally experienced many obstacles in attempting to integrate this ministry into those mission fields supported by the Church (see Chapter 8), I know it is not a time to give up. Just as the Church reaches out to mission fields in our communities and into other countries, the workplace mission field is no different. What an army of mission workers the Church can provide, as most of their members are already intimately a part of the workplace world! As one Church has adopted a parting phrase at the end of their worship services, "Church doesn't end on Sunday," so, too, do those in the body of the Church need to be encouraged to be full-time Christians.

With the help of this book and the testimonies provided herein, as well as the establishment and recognition of the WCFM, these efforts may be two small steps forward in gaining the attention and acceptance of those in the Church who will come to know the significance of God's plan for the workplace. Just as Bible study and other biblically related classes are commonly available to Church members and non-members alike, Churches can offer a time of fellowship and teaching to prepare participants for ministry work in their own workplace. Within these classes sharing and feedback about workplace circumstances, including both uplifting and difficult times, can serve to further develop and equip everyone. In the future, a formal study guide can be developed and made available to assist the leaders of these WCFM classes in the Church.

WCFM Sponsorship In Business Gathering Venues

Throughout my own thirty-plus years in the workplace, I have many times attended meetings or conferences pertaining to my own technical profession or business related activities. In most of these instances, the location of the gathering is different from where I normally live or work, causing me to travel and stay overnight. When traveling with co-workers, we would sometimes get to our destination in the late afternoon, allowing us time to check-in to the hotel and meet later for dinner together. As was also the case many times earlier in my career, instead of waiting in my room until the time for dinner, I would join my other traveling companions in the hotel lounge for drinks and socializing. During multiple day events, this same pre-dinner socializing would be repeated each day. The socializing was nice, but the consumption of alcoholic drinks and conversation that reflected the effects of the alcohol took a toll on me. As the years went by in my professional career, I matured in dealing with these traveling routines. It has gotten to a point, especially since I have become strong in my faith, that I refrain from these uncomfortable "happy hour" situations. Instead, I will go to my room and remain there to be by myself for the rest of the evening. I know that there has to be something better than this alternative antisocial behavior, and I'm sure there are other business travelers out there who feel the same way.

One idea that God has laid on my heart is to establish WCFM-sponsored hospitality rooms at various major hotel/conference center locations. The concept is to provide people alternatives to the happy hour choice, with a supportive and encouraging atmosphere of loving Christian fellowship. These locations would be open to anyone to take time out from the hectic and often stressful pace of meetings or conference activities. Complimentary non-alcoholic beverages and light snacks could be provided to add to the feeling of a comfortable place to rest, relax (both mentally and physically) and not be socially isolated. The prime time for making these hospitality rooms available would be around the happy hour time (e.g. 4-7 P.M.). Such rooms could also be open during the early morning hours (e.g. 7-9 A.M.) for people to start their day off right with Christian fellowship.

The logistics of providing these fellowship rooms seems relatively straightforward. Arrangements can normally be made to rent such rooms on an hourly basis. They can be staffed with one or two volunteers from local workplace fellowship groups in the immediate area who donate their time (e.g. an assigned once a month time slot). A local placard placed outside the door of the room can provide an invitation to all who may wish to enter. WCFM Web page resources can provide a listing of the locations where such fellowship rooms are located. Finally, the WCFM, local workplace fellowship groups, and Church outreach ministries can share in supporting the funding for the room rentals and refreshments. Such plans may seem like a lot to accomplish, but if the Lord intends for this to happen, it will.

A Bold Witness

In the course of my professional career, I have had a small amount of experience in speaking before groups of people, from business meetings to presenting technical papers at business conferences. These have been a limited number of occasions and have not allowed me to polish my speaking skills to any extent. I have a passion, however, to convey my message to others. Just as there are many people in the Bible who felt inadequate to speak in public, such as Moses, I also sense a similar anxious feeling. Since I know what God wants me to say, I will put my trust in the Lord. The Apostle Paul said it best: "I may not be a trained speaker, but I do have knowledge" (2 Corinthians 11:6). I am also prepared to step out of my comfort zone to present the passion of my heart before anyone who has an ear to listen. The last line of the daily prayer I have adopted provides me with the encouragement and determination to be bold in witnessing to others: "May my heart be sound in thy statutes, that I may not be ashamed" (Psalm 119:80).

11
A Calling

It appears to me that God's work in the workplace very much parallels His work in the Church. In fact, we are all one body of the Church wherever we are. If we are called to do His work in the workplace, we must be aware of the overall dynamic structure of the body of His Church as it extends into and functions within the workplace environment. His work can be accomplished at all levels of the workplace corporate structure, from the president or CEO (Chief Executive Officer) of a company, down through the entire rank and file of the organization. At the various individual corporate levels, there may be different approaches that can be taken within each of those levels to foster a ministry of Christian fellowship. From an overall perspective, however, two basic approaches emerge: from the *top down* and from the *bottom up*. This parallel dynamic in the Church is seen as those working from the top down to guide the group of believers, such as priests, pastors, elders, deacons, and laypersons, to name a few. In supportive contrast, Church emphasis on small groups starts at the bottom with the foundation of the Church, the people. This bottom up approach is the basis for WCFM.

From the *Top Down*

As a point of reference, I'd like to touch for a moment on those workplace conditions which support the Christian faith from the top down. As I do, let me be very clear that I consider these to be vital and essential ministry approaches, which make up part of God's plan. Every time I see an example of God working in this way, my spirit is lifted in the hope of seeing great things happen in His name.

Through the course of my exposure to various facets of top-level corporate support and endorsement of God in the workplace, I have noticed the following examples:

CEO's of Faith

C12, or Christian Twelve, is a national for-profit company founded in 1992 in the Tampa Bay (Florida) area by former Apollo Beach resident Lester "Buck" Jacobs. In a format patterned after Jesus and his twelve disciples, C12 members meet in groups of twelve to fifteen for one full weekday a month to share business advice, discuss salvation strategies, air family problems, and pray. About forty local chief executives belong to one of three C12 groups in the bay area. The local groups are among twenty-two C12 organizations across eleven states and Washington, D.C. (early 2004 statistics).

These C12 organizations are, indeed, examples of starting from the top. By the testimonies of various members of these groups, God is working in the lives of those who are part of these CEO level groups. The impact of these groups on the lives of those at the top management level is a great starting point. The next important step is to see how the changed characters of these individuals trickles down the corporate structure into the lower levels of management and, hopefully, into bottom echelons of the workplace.

Corporate Chaplains of America and Marketplace Ministries, Inc.

Both of these organizations are based on a similar concept of providing trained chaplains to subscribing businesses for personal contact with their employees. Although these are Christian based ministry services, their goal is to interrelate with all of a company's staff, regardless of each employee's religious or non-religious belief. In some business places this service falls under what is commonly referred to as an Employee Assistance Program or EAP.

These services are indeed a service to God's continuing work. Both organizations are highly organized with their own corporate structures and training programs. They openly publicize their emphasis on proselytizing in the workplace; that is, striving to convert persons from another religious belief to Christianity to the point of publishing statistics of their success in saving souls. The shortcomings of these services, however, are their limited exposure to all the potential workplaces. First, a business must be willing to accept this faith-based service into its workplace environment (i.e. having believers as part of its corporate management helps pave the path for this organization to happen). Secondly, there is a cost to the business, usually on a per person basis. Finally, the services, although promoting 24/7 availability, are not present in the workplace on a continuous basis, unless the size of a business staff requires a full-time chaplain.

Christian Based Businesses

Christian based businesses, as I am referring to here, exemplify a corporate commitment to the operation of their company on the basis of God's Word for living and working. Although these businesses do not require their entire staff to have a Christian belief, their principals of operation clearly demonstrate a Christian model to their staff. It is encouraging that with such a model ever-present in their workplace environment, a seed may be planted in the hearts and minds of non-believers to pursue their spiritual roots further.

One such business is The ServiceMaster Company. You may recognize the names of some of their core services, such as TruGreen Chem Lawn, Terminix, and Merry Maids. If you check out their corporate principals of operation, you will find their stated purpose to read as follows:

> The purpose of these Principles is to describe the manner in which the Company will be managed by or under the direction of its Board within the framework of its corporate objectives To Honor God In All We Do, To Help People Develop, To Pursue Excellence, and To Grow Profitably for the benefit of its shareholders.

The number one focus of The ServiceMaster Company honors God in all they do. Although The ServiceMaster Company does not directly reference God's Word in their corporate guidelines, it is clearly evident from reading their Code of Conduct, as prefaced by Chairman and CEO Jonathan P. Ward, that their emphasis and measure of success is to "Do the right thing." As the description of all of their corporate values and principles attest, they *are* the right values in the eyes of God.

Another business that exemplifies its honoring of God is the fast food convenience franchise Chick-fil-A, founded sixty years ago by Truett Cathy. As stated on its internet Web page, "Our official statement of corporate purpose says that we exist 'to glorify God by being a faithful steward of all that is entrusted to us and to have a positive influence on all who come in contact with Chick-fil-A'". One very visible testimony of this corporate purpose to the public world is that all of their outlets are closed on Sundays to honor God.

Strategic Christian Services
For those Christians who desire to better prepare themselves for management in the workplace, The Business Leadership School provided by Strategic Christian Services "is designed to equip owners, corporate executives, managers, and those aspiring to positions of leadership to engage the marketplace through the framework of the Scriptures." Their goals are:

1. To call and equip Christian leaders whose primary calling is to the marketplace, and who want to glorify God there through applied excellence, effective leadership, realistic evangelism, and faith-based decision making.

2. To help Christian leaders to build organizations and manage their most precious resource (their relationships) upon the foundations of God's Word.
3. To help energize, encourage, and facilitate local Churches as they organize, train, and release people to serve God where they work.
4. To network these trained servants and facilitate new local, national, and global opportunities for evangelism, business-based mission consulting teams, and capital creation.

There are other such Christian based organizations and corporately sponsored programs in the workplace. This list provides just a sampling of what is happening in those hidden fields, working from the top down.

<u>From the Bottom Up</u>

In contrast to the concept of *from the top down*, but in the integrated approach God has for His work to be done, the grass roots foundation of a Church in the *from the bottom up* approach is the people, because they know each other, care for one another, and worship the Lord in the unity of one body. This approach is characteristic of the early Churches, which met in believers' homes. As it probably was the case with most homes of that time and now, unless one was wealthy with a large house to accommodate many people, each Church consisted of a rather small group of people. It's interesting in today's time, with many Churches consisting of large congregations, how the emphasis is going back to meeting in small groups where intimate and personal relationships can flourish. So, too, the small groups in the workplace become the foundation formed by the people.

In most every workplace environment, the routine of daily activities fosters relationships with our co-workers. As we spend time in the workplace together, it is inevitable that we come to know one another on more than just a business relationship level. Our actions and emotions speak louder than words. Just by being together, we can not help but express our joys and sorrows of living a life on earth, whether from the inside or the outside of the workplace. Regardless if our own self-will is to maintain walls around us in order that we might erect to keep such things personal, it is almost impossible to completely hide our human condition. It is here that we gather together as a small group, like a family, to support and encourage each other in our common bond of service to our employer. This is the core of workplace fellowship.

Christian fellowship in the workplace is not intended to be in competition with or be treated separate from the Church. It *is* the Church. People who join in workplace fellowship are encouraged by their co-workers to find a Church family outside of the workplace. In addition, the gathering of people in the workplace from all different denominations reinforces that we are all one body. We are a unity of believers in one Church, which is Jesus Christ.

Now Is the Time

Christian fellowship in the workplace is a spiritual revival ready to explode. The beginning phases are already being seen around the country. But the moral decay of our society is a whirlpool that can suck believers in if we are not careful. The best way, in fact the only way, we can be strong against this threat is to be more intently focused on God and draw Him closer. As we have heard in the strategy of sports and the military, "The best defense is a good offense." Our best offense is definitely to have God in our lives at all times. Just as ministers have been saying that "Church doesn't end on Sunday," what better way can we know of God's presence and protection than by having Him in our lives during the time we spend in the workplace? So let's insure that Christian fellowship in the workplace continues to grow.

Workplace fellowship groups have already clearly demonstrated that they are a powerful tool in God's plan. Many people are familiar with the book entitled *The Purpose Driven Life* by Rick Warren, pastor of Saddleback Church in Lake Forest, California.[8] This book has been a source of spiritual renewal in this country and around the world. In his book, Warren outlines five purposes that God has for our lives: worship, fellowship, discipleship, ministry, and evangelism. All of these purposes are an essential part of living to bring glory and pleasure to God. Being part of a fellowship group in the workplace serves to fulfill these purposes in the following ways that have been outlined in this book:

Prayer ⇔ Worship
Family ⇔ Fellowship
Gathering ⇔ Discipleship
Outside the Walls ⇔ Ministry
Planting/Harvesting ⇔ Evangelism

At the beginning of my book, I shared the calling I received from the Lord to be part of His ministry in the workplace. At that particular time, it was somewhat difficult for me to grasp the significance of His plan for me. But now that I have served Him for several years, I know I am not in this service alone. Now is the time for other workers to receive a similar call to act. There is a reason each reader has received and read this book, whether he or she bought it for himself or another person gave or lent it. It was not by any accident or unplanned circumstance. It is God's plan for each of His children, just as everything else is according to His plan and His timing. Be ready to answer His call.

One initial question is probably, "Okay, I feel God's call and I'm ready, but what do I do next?" With God as our guide, the first thing we need to do is lift this readiness up in prayer to Him, seeking His direction and taking time to listen to Him. He *will* continue to reveal His plan for each of us. We need to understand that this experience may take us out of our comfort zone in dealing with people and our company environment. But we need to make a personal commitment to ourselves and God to be bold witnesses of faith in a sincere, caring, and loving way. Those of us with WCFM will be praying for and be ready to support each person in any way we can.

In sharing my own experiences, I feel that I am only one example of God's plan, as illustrated uniquely by my own workplace. Each of us must put our trust in Him for our own circumstances and use Him as our guide. These six key steps should assist us in following our calling:

1. Spend time with the Lord in **PRAYER**. This is the most powerful tool we have been given by God. Use it often.

2. **IDENTIFY** those people in the workplace who have revealed in any way that faith is a factor in their life. This might take the form of brief references they have made in the past about their Church activities, a need for prayer, or maybe you have seen them pray before they eat. Even comments others have made about someone's example of faith opens the door for dialog with them. Make a list and capture those things known about them regarding their faith.

3. Make a definite plan to **APPROACH** each of those identified individuals on your list, in a one-on-one setting. Share with them more about each other's faith. Express to them a desire to have more opportunities to get to know each other better in shared common bonds of faith.

4. **SCHEDULE** a first gathering. It can be as casual and comfortable as having lunch together with those people listed. Pick a location that is acceptable in the workplace environment. Regardless of how stringent the workplace environment, there will be a place and time workers can meet. Be open-minded and flexible, for if it is God's will, He will make it happen. Then in a personal way, invite those identified workers, one-on-one, face-to-face to meetings.

5. **PLAN** the group's time together. During the first several times together, just get to know one another better. After that a focus will reveal itself as a need of the group. Also, find one or more of the group gifted in leading discussions or topics of study. Let them use their gifts. Even if he or she wasn't the one to get the group started

in the first place, step back and let the Holy Spirit be alive and work among those in the group.

6. **MEET** together regularly. Be diligent to gather together on a routine basis. Don't ever give up meeting together. Distribution of written or verbal reminders of each periodic meeting to each one in the group encourages a continuity of togetherness. Continue to be reminded by Hebrews 10:25: not meeting together is exactly what the evil one wants to see happen. Challenges of schedules, meeting places, people's comments about the group, and company policies will occur. Remember, however, to be strong and persevere. Just be diligent and obedient to His calling, being reminded that "I can do all things through Christ who strengthens me" (Philippians 4:13). Nothing is impossible.

As I close, I would like to lift up all who take on this workplace ministry into the hands of the Father in prayer:

Gracious Heavenly Father,

You are an awesome God, a God of love. Your plan and purpose for our lives is perfect. You have brought forth the circumstances that have given us this calling to reach out to others a hand of fellowship in the workplace, in the name of your son, Jesus Christ. We thank you for this opportunity to serve you by serving others. May we be those faithful workers you are sending into your fields to gather your harvest of salvation. We praise you and give you thanks for everything, in the name of your most precious son, Jesus Christ. Amen.

ENDNOTES

1 Blackaby, Henry and Claude V. King. *Experiencing God*. Nashville: Life Way Press, 1990.
2 Promise Keepers, Denver, Colorado
3 Cymbala, Jim. *Fresh Wind, Fresh Fire*, Grand Rapids: Zonderyan Publishing House, Zonderyan, 1997
4 Rainey, Dennis and Barbara. *Moments Together for Couples*. Ventura: Gospel Light, 1996
5 *Merriam-Webster's Online*, © 2006, www.m-w.com.
6 *Merriam-Webster On-Line*. © 2000. www.m-w.com
7 Limbaugh, David. *"Persecution."* Washington D.C.: Regnery, 2003.
8 *The Purpose Driven Life*, Grand Rapids: Zondervan, 2002.